WE AIN'T MUCH, BUT WE'RE GETTIN' BETTER

A Memoir

Paul D. Waldrop

ISBN 979-8-89112-762-3 (Paperback)
ISBN 979-8-89112-763-0 (Digital)

Biography portrait by: Brandon Burk Photography
Developmental Edit by: Vince Font

Covenant Books
11661 Hwy 707
Murrells Inlet, SC 29576
www.covenantbooks.com

CONTENTS

INTRODUCTION

We Ain't Much but We're Gettin Better is the inspiring account of one person's journey from boyhood to manhood as he struggles to overcome the burdens of dyslexia and attention deficit disorder to become a remarkable success while at the same time suffering severe emotional and physical abuse from his parents. Rather than remaining the victim, Paul turned to faith in God and prayer to deal with the countless circumstances and problems he faced throughout life. In the end, he emerged triumphant and blessed.

CHAPTER 1

How to Pick Lemons

The first time my mother took me to church, I was three, and we were living in Las Cruces, New Mexico. She told a story about that first Sunday. After the meeting, most of the congregation had left, and my mother was visiting with someone near the rear of the chapel. With my mother's attention focused on her conversation, I was free to run back and forth between the pews.

My irreverence caught the attention of the bishop, who approached me and asked, "What's your name, little boy?"

With great pride, and to the bishop's dismay and my mother's horror, I replied, "My name is Paul Dam-it!"

Evidently, my mother expressed her frustration with my impetuousness, creativity, and constant surprises by addressing me quite often with "Paul, damn it!" She did so enough times that I really thought the "D" of my middle name stood for just that.

I can't remember a time in my life when I wasn't certain of the gospel of Jesus Christ. Soon after my mother started attending church, she met and married my stepfather. I was pleased to have a father, and I really liked him.

Not long after they married, and after my stepfather's graduation from New Mexico State University and ROTC, we left Las Cruces. During the next few years, we moved from New Mexico to Alabama, Maryland, Massachusetts, and New Hampshire, where we had the opportunity to visit many historic sites. It was an interesting time.

Those first few years of attending church were fun. In New Hampshire, we lived outside the town of Derry. Every Sunday, I helped set up the chairs for the morning meetings. It was one of the things I enjoyed the most. But my favorite part of attending church was the baptisms. Baptisms always took place in a stream that ran through one of the congregation member's farms, and everyone would attend. The stream was so cold that us kids couldn't bear to dip in our feet.

In the stream, there was a spot where someone had deepened and lined the streambed with smooth rocks. This was where the baptisms were held.

Afterward, everyone feasted on hamburgers, a variety of delicious side dishes, and fire-roasted sweet corn with the husks still on. These were wonderful celebrations that impressed upon me the importance of the occasion.

The summer after I turned seven, my family moved from Derry to Almo, Idaho, and then to Kearns, Utah, around Christmastime. The hardest thing for me was the fact I just didn't fit in, at school or at church. I thought the primary leader hated me. But despite all the disapproval and disappointment, I loved primary and attended regularly. I loved learning about God, Jesus Christ, and his gospel.

Many of the children in the congregation had been there for most of their lives. I was an outsider in a place where they'd not had to deal with many newcomers. I'd also come from a divorced family, and there weren't many people like us in that area. I was very aware of how different I was and how it separated me from the other children.

I tried to be reverent and obedient, but I seemed to always find a way to blow it and get into trouble. It might be speaking out of turn, blurting out the answer to a question asked of another child, or just constantly fidgeting and moving. I may have had "two little hands folded snugly and tight," but not for long. I wanted to be able to stand in front of the whole primary and hold the reverence banner, but to do so, I had to be the best example of "reverence," and I never got to hold the banner.

Everyone has things they enjoy that have no relevance to the gospel. For me, that was lemons—the most delicious fruit the world has to offer. I loved its sourness, its tartness, and its unique flavor. The smell of the lemon is always refreshing and enticing.

One winter, when I was eight, I shoveled snow to earn money. After one successful day of shoveling, I walked to the grocery store and bought ten lemons. I took them home, cut them up, got the salt-shaker, and ate the entire lot while watching TV.

I think I almost killed myself that night. I was sure sick, but my love of lemons was unscathed. To this day, I never eat more than two or three lemons at a time. When I order a drink in a restaurant, it's always water with a lemon wedge. I also order lemon wedges as the dressing for my salad.

Knowing how to pick lemons was one of the most treasured bits of knowledge I've ever learned. This most valued information was given to me at the tender age of nine—the year Sister Labrum became my primary class teacher. It was she who, when she learned of my obsession with lemons, took me to the grocery store and taught me how to pick out the lemons that would give me the most for my money. The secret was simple: smooth and shiny lemons have the thinnest skin and the most meat. Those with rough, bumpy skin have thick skin and less meat.

I thought Sister Labrum was wonderful for taking me to the store and teaching me such a thing. To tell the truth, I fell in love with Sister Labrum. I remember watching her as she taught the class and thinking how wonderful, kind, and caring she was. She had a son the same age as me who was in my class, and she treated every student in the same caring way she did her own son.

I felt jealous of her son. I wished I were her son too. The one thing she did that affected me the most was making me believe she really liked me. I think she saw me differently than most of the other teachers and leaders. I felt valued by her. I decided that I would try my hardest to behave better in class and during the opening of primary. I would have done anything Sister Labrum asked of me. I didn't want to disappoint her in any way.

One of the things the primary leaders did to encourage the children to behave was to vote every month for the most reverent boy and girl and award them with a book of scripture, a copy of the New Testament: Large Type printed especially for children. The awards were announced and presented in front of the entire primary. It was a great honor to receive the award.

I will never forget that primary for the first week of November 1963. I went into the meeting and sat with my class. Opening exercises progressed just as they always had. Finally, it came time to announce the most reverent girl and boy. They announced the name of the girl, and she went up and received her award. Then came the boy's turn. They announced the name, and no one responded.

Sister Labrum nudged me and said, "Paul, they called your name."

I said, "What, me? But I'm not reverent."

I was astounded and confused. Sister Labrum urged me to get up and receive the award. I did so in a dazed state, feeling embarrassed and undeserving. As we separated for classes, the other children even teased me for receiving the award. I felt hurt.

Not long after, Sister Labrum took my award, opened it to a blank page, and wrote:

Dear Paul,

> *Congratulations on being voted the most reverent boy in primary for the month of October. I am very proud of your efforts, and I am very glad you are a member of my Blazer class. Try hard for another award.*

Love,
Sister Phyllis J. Labrum

I don't think I heard another word she or anyone else said for the rest of class. When I got home, I showed the award and message to my mother, stepfather, and adopted sister. My adopted sister was also in primary at the time. My parents congratulated me and were encouraging, but not my sister. I don't remember exactly what she said, but as usual, it wasn't nice, kind, or supportive.

I was so hurt and angry that I took a pen and scribbled over Sister Labrum's sweet message. Then I threw the book in the trash. After a few minutes, I retrieved the book and read the message again. Both it and the award meant a great deal to me, so I decided to keep it.

To this day, I still treasure the award and keep it prominently displayed on my fireplace mantle. Occasionally, I open it and am still moved by Sister Labrum's words and encouragement.

I wonder what she had to do to get the other teachers and leaders to vote for me. Did she tell a white lie? Other times I wonder if maybe, by some wild chance, I had actually earned the award. One thing's for sure: as a nine-year-old boy, I worked a lot harder at being reverent and behaving because I knew she genuinely cared for me.

Looking back, when I try to remember a wonderful gospel truth I learned in Sister Labrum's class, I can think of nothing. All I remember is that she was a caring, loving, and wonderful teacher who will always hold a dear spot in my heart. I'm most grateful for the blessing of a teacher who knew how to pick lemons.

CHAPTER 2

Blue Pass

It was February 1966. Just three months before my twelfth birthday. I lay in bed and sobbed into my pillow to muffle the sound of my cries, staring at the shadow on the floor the moonlight cast though the window. It was a large window with small panes of glass that cast a grid pattern on the floor.

I'd never felt such fear in my life. I was afraid to move or make the slightest sound, even breathe. In the corner, several beds over from mine, slept a huge, ugly bald man. He had a look that sent chills though me. They said he'd killed people with an ax. There was another man who talked to himself all the time and still another who just smiled constantly with a crazy look on his face. There were a few kids there too. All the kids were older than me, but it helped to know they were there. My mother had committed me to the Utah State Mental Hospital in Provo because I'd been diagnosed with attention deficit disorder (ADD).

As I lay there crying, I prayed to God, asking him why I had to be there and begging him to send me back home. I promised God, over and over and over again, that I would be a better boy. I would behave and do everything I was told. I would try harder than I ever had if he would just let me go home.

It wasn't for my lack of trying. I'd tried hard, but nothing worked. I went to church every week and tried to do what the teacher said I should. I tried to do what my mother told me, but all I did was make her angrier. At school, I increasingly aggravated my teacher and the principal. I struggled with every element of life. I just couldn't do anything right.

At one point, they sent me to a tutor several times a week to learn my vowels, grammar, and spelling. I'll never forget the tutor's frustration with me as she had me repeat my vowels. I could never get things straight. It all seemed jumbled to me, and half the time, things seemed backward. I was just plain stupid. I knew it, and even worse, every kid in my class knew it. They called me meathead. It wasn't long before the kids at church also started calling me the same.

At Sunday school, I was taught to turn the other cheek, to be more kind to others, and not to fight. I had been in a lot of fights, and I knew that I needed to stop. One day on my way home from the tutor's, three boys from my class caught me and started beating me up. I refused to fight back. I wanted to be better and do what I'd been taught in Sunday school. I ended up on the ground with my arms protecting my head while they hit and kicked me black and blue.

That wasn't the worst of it. The boys told all the other kids how I'd refused to fight back, that I'd just laid there while they beat me up. Everyone laughed and gave me a new nickname: Sally.

Things at home were just as bad, even worse. My mother was constantly angry with me, always calling me names and telling me that I was ugly, stupid, and worthless. That I was just like my horrible father. She whipped, hit, and kicked me for almost everything. If I left a speck of food on a dish and went to bed, she'd come into my room and hit me with a broom handle until I was awake. Usually, I would fall out of bed and crawl down the hall into the kitchen, where she continued to whack me until I rewashed every dish, dirty or not.

My adopted sister would steal money from my mother's purse. Even though she got away with it, she told my mother I'd stolen it. My mother would fly into a rage and beat me until I could hardly move. The worst part of it was that later, when she discovered I hadn't stolen her money, my mother would say, "Well, you did *something* to deserve it."

If I didn't clean my room or closet, she would beat me with her fists or hit me with whatever she could get her hands on. Other times, she'd throw me to the floor and stomp on me. Once, when I left wire hangers on my closet floor, she knocked me down and stomped my head into the hangers until they drew blood. Then she took a belt to me for making such a fuss and for bleeding everywhere.

One time, she knocked me to the floor and sat on top of me, holding me down. Then she used my ears as handles as she bashed my head into the tiled concrete floor. I remember things going purple then black. I came to sometime later with my mother still on top of me, only now she was slapping my face as hard as she could to wake me up. My head flopped from side to side with every slap.

"How dare you scare me like that, you little sh——!" she screamed.

My home life was pure hell. But being in the state hospital was even worse. I would have given anything to go back home. I felt so ashamed that I wanted to die. There were times I thought of killing myself. On a couple of occasions, I tried to hang myself in my closet. The only thing that stopped me was the knowledge that God had forbidden it.

My sixth-grade teacher had taught at the youth center at the Utah State Hospital and told my mother how it had helped other kids. That was all my mother needed to hear. She was certain it was right for me.

My mother was a hypochondriac, not only for herself but for me as well. I can't count the number of times she either heard or read about a malady vexing some poor kid and became instantly sure that was what was wrong with me. She took me to this or that clinic, this or that doctor, this or that hospital, including the children's hospital in Salt Lake City, for numerous tests and evaluations. She was positive there was something wrong with me. Now I was in this horrible place, and she was certain it was right for me.

It took several weeks to become accustomed to being at the hospital. I felt I didn't belong, and I was confused about why I was there at all. What made things even worse was the fact the hospital started me on medication—Dexedrine, I think. It was a triangular orange pill, what they called an "upper," a type of speed. It was supposed to help kids with ADD, but it didn't help me. They said I was "bouncing off the walls" and described me as being "overwound." All I really remember was that I couldn't sleep or sit still, even for a moment.

Eventually, they changed my medication to what they called a "downer." I don't remember the name, but I do recall the effect. For the first week or so, I was barely able to stay awake and usually just sat staring at the wall. The doctors lowered the dose, and I stayed on that pill regimen for a while.

Once I settled into the routine at the youth center, it wasn't too bad. I wasn't beaten every day by my mother, and I was even able to take part in several arts-and-crafts projects. I made ceramics, enameled trinkets from flat metal sculptures, and did some leatherwork.

All the juvenile residents were assigned what we called the "White House." Each morning, a counselor named Dennis would escort all the kids to the youth center for school and counseling. I really liked Dennis.

After a couple of months, my issue of not getting along well with others resurfaced. One day, Dennis called a meeting with all the youths in the recreation room. Apparently, the older kids had complained that I was tagging along with them too much. I was unprepared for what took place next.

Unbeknownst to me, my mother had had one of her "long talks" with Dennis and the other youth counselors, advisers, and staff. In keeping with her nature, she'd presented herself as wonderful while painting me as a troubled "bad boy" who'd been mistreated horribly by my father and life itself.

As a result, I was the topic of the meeting in the recreation room. Dennis began the meeting by talking about how we should all become acquainted with one another and get to know people before criticizing and complaining. He went on to explain that he wanted to share my life story and the things that I'd experienced with everyone.

I was mortified. I wanted to run and hide, but, of course, I couldn't. First, Dennis told the group how when I was a baby my father had spanked and slapped me when I cried in an effort to toughen me up. He told everyone that when I was three months old, my father had tossed me into the air and my head had hit the ceiling fan. Of course, I'd cried loudly, so my father had taken my diaper off and spanked me harshly. Next, Dennis went on to tell everyone how when I was eighteen months old, my father had kidnapped me. According to my mother, she didn't know where I was for a full six months.

Even though I was only eighteen months old, I remember the day he took me. We were at the Waldrop Homestead west of Deming visiting Granny and Grandpa Waldrop. My father and uncle Charlie were there. Earlier that day, I'd ridden with Uncle Charlie on the tractor.

My mother and Grandma Schesslur, her mother, came to pick me up from the visit. I remember we were all out in front of the house near the evergreen windbreak trees. Suddenly, Grandma Schesslur was swinging a two-by-four at my father. He caught it, and the next thing I knew, they each had a two-by-four and were hitting each other with them. My mother stepped in and joined the fight.

The next thing I recall, my father grabbed me, put me in a car, and sped away. I looked out the back window and watched dust clouds rise from the road. He took me to Lemon Grove, California, for about three months. Then he took me to Tucson, Arizona, and left me with friends. I was with them for about three months.

I still have memories of my time there. They often put me in a playpen outside and didn't feed me well. I remember being very hungry and climbing out of the playpen, finding an anthill, trying to eat the ants, and screaming because they were stinging and biting me.

Sometime after that, Granny and Grandpa Waldrop came to visit me in Tucson. They discovered me suffering from serious malnutrition and covered with impetigo, a skin strep infection from all the ant stings. Granny called the authorities and had me returned to my mother but not before spending several weeks in the hospital recovering.

Next, Dennis told the story about how when I was five and living with my mother and stepfather in Huntsville, Alabama, I came down with listeria and wasn't expected to live. One night after playing in the next-door neighbor's pigeon coop, I began to feel ill and went to my mother's room.

Once I said "Mommy, I feel sick," everything went black. Three days later, I came to in the hospital after being in a coma with a high temperature. While in the coma, the nurses gave me alcohol baths to cool me down. Sometime during the three days, the doctors diagnosed me with listeria and said it was very unlikely I'd survive. At that time, there were no treatments or cures for listeria, and only one in three or four hundred thousand people survived it. During my time in the coma, my stepfather called the church elders to give me a blessing. Three hours after the blessing, I awoke from the coma and recovered completely.

Finally, Dennis told everyone in the meeting about my struggles in school and how I'd gotten into numerous fights and didn't get along well on the "outside." Dennis didn't know about the mistreatment, name-calling, and beatings my mother gave me nearly every day or how when I was a toddler she'd go on dates and leave me home alone. Before she left, she tied me up and put me in bed with the sheets and blankets tucked in tightly around me. Then she put heavy chairs and large toys on top of me and warned me not to get out of bed. I always found a way to get loose for which she harshly punished me when she returned. Of course, my mother would have never shared or admitted such things.

When the session was over and Dennis was done telling everyone all about my life, I was sobbing uncontrollably. I felt completely exposed as if my guts had been ripped out and laid on the floor for everyone to see. I don't know if it was embarrassment, self-pity, or just humiliation—but it was one of the most emotionally wrenching experiences of my life. I was glad when it was over. But I was even more glad when afterward, things seemed to settle down.

There was an older woman who was severely brain damaged that was a resident on our floor. The story was that once she had been a professor at a university, but she'd had a habit of cursing and getting angry. To help her, she'd been subjected to electric shock treatment, which had caused her brain damage.

She was a funny character who often walked around without her teeth, in her underwear with her robe loosely tied. When we weren't in class, we spent most of our time in the recreation rooms, playing pool, shuffleboard, and other games. Some of the time was spent doing homework. Often, she would come into the recreation room smacking her gums, stand with her hands behind her back and her tummy sticking out, and just look at us. As bad as it sounds, it was awfully hard not to laugh at her.

The thing I liked most about her, though, was that if she walked in on us while we were doing homework, we could ask her almost any question and she'd know the answer. She could spell as well as any dictionary. We all thought it was a sad thing they'd done to her.

Several of the people and kids came, went, and came back again. Sometimes, the hospital organized field trips where we as a group would do fun or interesting things. Most evenings, under the supervision of a counselor, we were allowed as a group onto the grounds. There was an amphitheater made from river rock behind the White House. It was an interesting place with many nooks and crannies that proved a relaxing place to just hang out.

I was allowed to go home and visit most weekends. Often, my stepfather would take me fishing, hunting, or camping. He'd bought me a shotgun for my twelfth Christmas, and sometimes we would go rabbit hunting. He was a good thing in my life, offering an example of normality. My mother would sometimes leave or threaten to leave him. My greatest fear was that she actually would. I will always appreciate him driving all the way to Provo to pick me up and delivering me back on Sunday evenings.

As the months dragged on, things became routine—even all the crazy things going on with the kids or residents of the hospital. For the first eight or nine months of my stay, I felt like a kid forced to be somewhere I didn't want to be. I hated what my mother and the hospital were doing to me. I often sat and watched TV and felt sorry for myself, believing that everything and everyone was against me. I had no personal power or control. I was angry, but I couldn't do anything about it.

But as my thirteenth birthday neared, I decided I was tired of always having somebody always looking over me, telling me what to do or not to do. I was tired of never being alone. I was tired of being forced to take medications that I didn't feel I needed. I was tired of being surrounded by people who had no grasp of reality. I didn't want to live with mentally ill people anymore. I didn't want to be counted as one of them. I decided that I had to get control over my own life.

The hospital had several types of passes that allowed residents to leave the building. Although I was too young to qualify for a pass that allowed me to go into the city to work or shop or visit, I was old enough for a pass that allowed me to go unsupervised onto the hospital grounds. They called this pass a Blue Pass. The idea of going where I wanted with nobody else around, even though limited to the grounds, was appealing. I decided to do what it took to get a Blue Pass.

I visited with Dennis, the doctors, and the administrators and told them I wanted to get a Blue Pass. Although I was told that no one as young as me had ever gotten one, there were no rules prohibiting it as long as I met all the requirements, and I was welcome to try. I knew they were skeptical, but the one thing I was known for was being extremely stubborn and hardheaded. Even my mother sometimes called me Cannonball Paul. I had to be in order to survive her.

The first thing I had to do was stay out of trouble. I was known to mouth back, be rebellious, and not listen, but I knew I had to change my thinking and behavior if I was going to get a Blue Pass. In another few weeks, I would be there for a full year. I knew I had to do something about my attitude. I watched other people, and I saw that those who got along the best with others were simply agreeable.

I decided that life was like a game. There were rules to life, and when followed, things fell into place.

Most of the teachers, counselors, and doctors were encouraging. I often asked how I was improving and if I was getting closer to getting a Blue Pass. Before, I would react or get involved when other kids acted out or got into trouble. But with my new goal, I couldn't afford to do either, so I kept my distance. The more distant from those incidents, the better I felt. Things were going much better for me. I was feeling good.

As my thirteenth birthday approached, my anticipation of getting the pass was intense. I'd put everything in my soul into behaving and getting along. Sometimes, the other kids would say to me, "Paul, you're doing so well, how come?" When I told them I was working on getting a Blue Pass, most would wish me good luck. I was all but certain that it would happen.

When the day came for the meeting for my review, I was excited and overcome with fear. What would life be like if they didn't allow me to have a Blue Pass? I couldn't imagine going on. Everything was riding on getting that pass. I had honestly done my best. I had nothing more.

I was called into a meeting room at the youth center before Dennis, a couple of teachers, and a doctor. They said I had met all the requirements and that I'd done better than anyone expected. But as I listened, I could tell they weren't going to give me a Blue Pass.

Choking back tears, I asked, "Are you going to give me a Blue Pass?"

They answered, "No."

To everyone's surprise, I exploded into tears and loud moans. My world was destroyed! Immediately, they began to console me. They told me to stop crying, that I had misunderstood, and that I needed to listen to them. There was more. They said that I wasn't going to be receiving a Blue Pass because I was going to be released.

I'd never considered the prospect of being released. I knew my mother, and I knew she would never choose to let me go back home. But the counselors, doctors, and teachers all told me they were going to force her to take me home. They said it might take a few weeks, but there was no question that I was going to be released. All I had to do was to continue behaving and avoiding conflict.

I did just as they counseled, and several weeks later, my mother and stepfather came to pick me up. It was obvious the last thing my mother wanted was to take me home, but she had no choice. She let me know in no uncertain terms that she thought this was a mistake and it wouldn't be long before I was back in the hospital where I belonged.

But I knew differently. I would never be back because I had learned several important lessons. The first was that my mother was not as all-powerful as she thought. The second was that feeling sorry for myself didn't help things. It actually hurt. I'd spent my life feeling sorry for myself, fighting the system, and losing at every turn. Finally, I'd learned to take personal responsibility and make my own choices—the right choices—and because of that, life would reward me. I had learned the rules of life. And I learned that if you play by those rules, you win.

CHAPTER 3

Meeting Father

I had gone by my stepfather's surname since I was three years old. I knew I had a different last name, but I didn't know what it was. Sometimes, when my mother wasn't home, I'd sneak into her bedroom. In the bottom drawer of a large chest was where she kept all the family photos and papers. The drawer was filled nearly to the top. I enjoyed digging through the piles of photographs, latching onto one, and reminiscing.

One day, while enjoying one of my intrusions into Mother's drawer of pictures, I pulled up a copy of my birth certificate. There was my full name. I tried to pronounce my real surname but struggled. As I was studying my birth certificate, my mother pulled into the driveway. I quickly put things back in order and shut the drawer then ran to the front room and acted as if I'd been watching TV. I didn't get caught.

As the days wore on, I struggled to remember my real last name but was having a hard time. I sneaked back to the drawer several times, searching for and finding my birth certificate. Each time, I'd look at my surname, spell it out, and try to commit it to memory. My father's full name was there also.

By the time I was thirteen, I began to wonder what my real father was like. I had only heard horrible stories about him from my mother. According to her, there was not one good thing about him, and at times, she would tell me that I was just as bad as he was. She told me how much I looked like him and that I would end up just like him: "No good." She also told me that she'd had to take me away to protect me from him, but knowing my mother, I didn't believe anything she said.

Just after my fourteenth birthday, my mother told me that she was considering sending me off to live with my real father. She said it was because I was too much trouble and because of the problems I'd created. As she spoke, she held her nose arrogantly in the air, looking to one side and shaking her head.

She wanted me to beg her not to send me away. But to her surprise, I expressed interest in the idea. As much as I enjoyed seeing her taken aback by my willingness, the fact was I really wanted to know my father. I wanted to know for myself what kind of person he was.

After several phone conversations and as soon as school was out for the summer, I was taken to Salt Lake City airport and put on an airplane. It was exciting. This would be my first airplane ride and the first time I traveled anywhere alone. I even enjoyed the large mosaic of the world on the floor of the airport terminal. On the plane, I took a window seat so I could see everything. It was amazing to see things get smaller as we gained altitude.

I was both excited and scared to meet my father. The last memory I had of him was when he came to visit me when I was three years old and living with my grandmother in Las Cruces. He showed up in a big black car with several of his army friends and asked to see me. My mother refused to let him see me and shut all the doors and curtains so he couldn't see inside. I got into trouble with my mother because I kept peeking through the curtains and trying to see him. He left, and I didn't see, speak, or hear from him again until my solo trip to visit him.

I had memories of Granny and Grandpa and was excited to see them as well. I expected that my father, stepmother, and their children would be at the Silver City airport to pick me up. But as the airplane taxied to a stop, I saw a crowd of people. Not only had my father and his family shown up to greet me, but Granny and Grandpa were there, too, including several of my uncles, aunts, and cousins.

It was overwhelming. I didn't know what to think. At the same time, it felt wonderful. I was part of a big family. I will always remember that moment of feeling valued by so many people. It was nothing I'd ever experienced before.

My father and stepmother were renting a small house on the east side of Deming across from a golf course. There wasn't much room, and I had to sleep on the couch, but I really didn't care. I was just glad to be there.

I learned I had two half-sisters and a toddler half-brother that I'd never met. It was hard to see everyone as family. To me, they were strangers. I knew this man was my father, yet at the same time, I didn't know him at all.

My father and stepmother had an old hand-highlighted photograph of me when I was around three years old. They had told their kids my nickname was Buddy, but I didn't like the name and refused to let them call me that. The last thing I wanted was for them to define who I was. I'd already been defined by my mother, and I hated it.

I'm sure my attitude was much of the problem. This place didn't feel like home, and these people didn't feel like family. I wanted them to feel like family, and I'm sure they wanted to feel the same. There were honest efforts from everyone, but there were so many differences, and nothing was familiar or comfortable.

Out back of the little house, they kept chickens and two pigs. One pig was a black-and-white Hampshire barrow named Arnold. The other was a big red Duroc sow that was about to have piglets. There was also a big garden. We were extremely poor, so to supplement the family income, we sold squash from the garden and the weaner pigs. I enjoyed helping with the animals and the garden and going with my father when he went to sell them.

One of the jobs my father worked was to drive a truck twice a week between Deming and Los Palomas, Mexico. We would leave Deming with bins of plastic toy parts. In Los Palomas, we delivered the toy parts to a building where twenty or thirty girls between the ages of twelve to sixteen worked assembling the parts into completed toys like trucks or cars. I really enjoyed meeting and flirting with all the girls. I could speak a few words of Spanish, enough to say hello and ask their names. I didn't understand most of what they were saying, but it was great fun seeing them.

I remember seeing the Los Palomas town sheriff. He was scary at the same time very cool. He was dressed just like an Old West sheriff right out of a Western movie with a black hat, a black holster, shiny cartridges, and a big six-shooter on his hip. On our return trip to Deming, we delivered the assembled toys back to the warehouse where we'd picked up the parts.

We made these trips for about four weeks, and then my father got a better-paying job working with the Billy Carrol Construction Company. My father was a heavy equipment operator and a good mechanic. He was friends with Billy, and it wasn't long before I was allowed to go to work with him as his helper. I really enjoyed helping him, and the rest of the summer, we spent overhauling Caterpillar D-8 bulldozers.

Not long after working with my father, both he and Billy said that I could do as much work as a grown man and that I was stronger than many. I liked hearing that. It felt good to know I was doing well at something.

I enjoyed working with my father. He was tough, but I learned from him. Sometimes, he wasn't patient with me and expected me to know things I didn't, like to be ready with tools when he needed them. He could be quick, rough, and hard with his anger and backhand.

His habit was to ask for a "doohickey." That's not actually the word he used, but it would be improper to use the word he actually used, which was a Spanish curse word. I quickly learned that "doohickey" meant whatever it was he needed to perform the job at the moment he asked for it. It might have been an open/box end wrench of a particular size, a screwdriver, a crescent wrench, vice grips, or some other random tool.

Through this, I developed what I called a "32nd eye," which meant I could look at a bolt head or nut and know the size within 1/32 of an inch. The price of not knowing was painful. My father's tactics were tough, but he did teach me to watch what was going on and predict what would be needed. It was an ability that served me well over the years.

At the end of the summer, I started eighth grade at Deming Junior High School. Several of my cousins went to school there as well, including my cousin Everett who was a year older than me and one of my favorite people. This was the first time I'd gone to a school where I had family. It was nice to feel like I was part of a community where people were part of me and I was part of them. Some of the kids introduced themselves to me as second cousins. It was an interesting time when almost everybody and everything was new.

In Deming schools, Waldrops had a reputation for being the toughest people. I was aware of the reputation, but I didn't see myself as contributing to it. Back home in Kearns, most people thought of me as a wimp and called me Sally. I think I saw myself as a wimp as well.

About two weeks after school started, I was riding home on the bus. At the same time, there was a noticeably big kid riding the bus too. I probably wouldn't have noticed him if he didn't have his arm around an attractive girl. It wasn't long before he started an argument with me and wanted to fight. I think it was all about showing his girlfriend that he was tough and could beat up the dumb-looking kid.

He was seventeen, a junior, and much bigger than me. I complained to the bus driver, and she forced the three of us off the bus. There we were in the middle of a dirt road, the big kid, his girlfriend, and me. I tried to tell him I didn't want to fight, but that just encouraged him. He started hitting and kicking me. When he was finished, I was lying in the dirt, and he was mocking me. I picked myself up, dusted myself off, and walked the three blocks home.

When my father met me in the dirt alley that led to our house, I could see he was upset. "What happened?" he asked.

"He beat—" I began, but before I could say another word, my father knocked me to the ground with a crushing blow to my neck and shoulder. Then he began kicking and pounding me.

All the while, he yelled at me, telling me I was a Waldrop and that "Waldrops don't let people beat them up." He said that if I ever let someone beat me up again, he'd kick my butt ten times as badly as this. He finally stopped, and once again, I picked myself up and dusted myself off.

I thought a lot about the incident. I had no doubt that my father would do exactly as he said he would.

As fate would have it, two weeks later, I encountered the same kid again on the bus. This time, he had his arm around a different girl. Just as he had before, he started an argument and wanted to fight. Again I protested, and again the bus driver forced me off the bus with them. I told the kid again that I didn't want to fight. He just laughed.

Then I told him he wasn't going to win this fight, that I'd be the one walking away and leaving him hurt and on the ground. He laughed and took a swing at me, but things were different this time. I ducked and tore into him with everything I had. I punched and kicked him, and it wasn't long before he was curled up into a ball on the ground, moaning.

I turned and walked the three blocks home. This time when my father met me in the dirt alley that led to the house, he asked me "What happened?"

"I whipped him," I said, "and left him lying in the dirt."

"Good," he said.

That kid never bothered me again.

I'd won fights in the past, but I only fought as hard as it took to get the other guy to quit fighting. In this incident, my father taught me three things. The first was that winning is more attitude than ability. Second, if you're going to fight, fight like hell. And third, convince them they never want to risk a fight with you again!

As the school year progressed, things were going well, and I had several friends. I was getting by with fair grades. It might have been better if I'd stayed in Deming with my father. There was a lot I liked about living with him. But it still didn't feel like home. As Christmas grew closer, I grew more homesick for Kearns, snow, and more familiar surroundings, and I abruptly decided to return home.

It didn't take long for things to deteriorate once I got back to Kearns. Spending time with my stepfather was good, but almost any interaction with my mother was pure hell and misery.

By Thanksgiving of the following year, I had arranged to return to Deming again and live with my father.

CHAPTER 4

Why These Families?

There is little that exceeds the value of family. The mere living with and among one's family molds an individual's security, value, education, and self-image. Physical appearance, size, and intellect are the results of genetics and are passed on from generation to generation. The family can and should be a refuge from the influences and perils of the world. As a youth, when I watched other families that had been built for generations upon love, respect, and understanding, my heart yearned for the same.

My life started without the influence of correct principles or the influence of truth. For the most part, I am disappointed in my grandparents, with the exception of my paternal grandmother who during her life was as Christlike as anyone I've ever known. My paternal grandfather was hardworking, an elder, and a faithful member of the church of his choice. On several occasions, he expressed to me his disappointment in me for not being a member of the same church. While I think it kept him from letting himself really get to know me, he did tolerate my visits, and I think he knew it was better for me to visit with him and Granny than be with my father.

My maternal grandfather deserted from the US Army during World War I. He abandoned his family, and he was a con man and philanderer. My maternal grandmother was, to say the least, odd. She was obsessed with cleanliness. I can still remember as a small child taking Lysol or chlorine bleach baths that burned my eyes and stung my skin. She passed away at the age of seventy-three, living a shameful life, which I won't discuss.

My mother and father were the expected products of such examples. My father had a temper that edged on homicidal, and he barely supported his family. My mother could hold her own in any conflict and was never able to manage her emotions. Even though my mother was foreign to self-confidence and security—having been abused and abandoned by her father and mistreated by her mother—she had two virtues that led her to "give me better than she got."

Those two virtues were "a belief in God" and "courage." Her "belief in God" led her to seek out and attend church. Her courage led her to marry my stepfather and live among people that were drastically different from her. Doing those two things provided me with fleeting glimpses of normalcy. Don't get me wrong, life with my parents was torturous, especially as seen through the eyes of a child. Yet as a man, looking back, I see some good in a few of her choices.

When I was three years old, just after she started attending church, my mother met and married the man that became my stepfather. My stepfather was a good man who was raised in a kind and loving family. He was a good example of living the gospel, and I loved him dearly. When we were together as a family, there was a sense of security and belonging—and with the tumultuous early life I'd experienced, his stabilizing influence was a blessing.

I was immensely proud of my stepfather's name. I can remember when I was four or five waiting in the car at a military base commissary in Huntsville, Alabama, while my mother and stepfather bought groceries. A boy in the next car rolled down his window and asked me my name. Proudly, I told him my name was Paul Kimber, and he began to make fun of me, chanting "Timber!" and falling over laughing.

I was furious! I got out of the car to try to make him stop, but he was unfortunately safe in his car. Not long after my attempt to straighten out this misguided boy, my parents returned and caught me in the act of defending the family name. No matter how I tried to explain the situation, I was in trouble—I wasn't supposed to get out of the car!

My sweet step-grandmother was a good influence in my life. She was a widow for over fifty years, My step-grandfather had passed away while serving a mission. She lived to be ninety-seven years old and served little children for over four decades. We were all immensely proud of her.

My heartbreaking disappointment with both my stepfather and step-grandmother was that when I was alone with them, I felt valued and treated as one of the family. But when in the company of uncles, aunts, or cousins, I was treated as a stepchild by everyone. I guess it was a foreign concept for them to deal with such a situation. It affected me deeply and caused me sadness. Although I was going by their surname, I had no standing and no real belonging to the Kimber family.

By the age of fifteen, I had been in and out of my mother and stepfather's home numerous times and had returned a second time to live with my real father and stepmother in Deming. I worked on a 160-acre farm after school, on weekends, and throughout summer from before sunrise to well after dark. I spent many hours alone and in prayer. It got to the point where I talked with God about everything as if God were right there next to me in open conversation.

One night in the spring of 1970, I was in despair. I was overcome with sadness. I felt deeply alone. I didn't fit into any place on earth. I thought of the many other young men I knew who had families that loved them and wanted them. Even though I'd made many mistakes, I wanted to do the right things in life.

There was a dirt irrigation tank in the center of the farm on the north end that was about eight feet high. I walked to the top of the tank and sat down. I could sharply hear all the desert sounds. It was very dark, and the night sky was starlit in magnificence. I felt so small and insignificant. I gazed into the stars, and with tears in my eyes, I began to tell God how I didn't seem to belong anywhere and that I wanted to belong. I told him I could see he had blessed so many kids with secure and loving families, and those young men didn't even seem to care.

I asked God why he had blessed other kids and not me. Why had he put me into families where I didn't belong, where there was so much anger, hurt, and pain? As I sat looking into the night, a calming voice spoke to me. The voice was deep, crisp, clear, and penetrating.

It said, "You were put into these families to establish a righteous lineage unto me and bring your forbearers into the gospel through temple work."

This message was of foundational importance to me. With this message, there was now meaning to all the pain, mistreatment, loneliness, and insecurity I'd experienced. For the first time, I felt important in the scheme of the family.

It was now clear to me. I was the one who, for my family, was called to link the past, present, and future together in the gospel. I was the one called to function as a filter, straining out hate, anger, and resentment, to push aside all the false principles, concepts, selfish traditions, and mistreatment. I was to somehow replace those habits, traditions, and concepts with love, kindness, and respect. I was to secure the truths, promises, and blessings for my family.

A sense of security that I had never felt before came over me. For the first time, I felt that I could face whatever came my way, and I was determined to do so. I felt a greater desire to live the gospel. At last, I had purpose and value.

About two weeks later, I was allowed to visit my maternal great-aunt Lela in El Paso, Texas. Lela defined the word "great." She seemed to always have deep wisdom and understanding, and she commanded respect from all she knew. She was a lady who knew most of the "dirty laundry" in my mother's family but didn't seem to condemn anyone. She drove the almost two-hundred-mile round trip from El Paso to Deming to pick me up for the visit.

I was excited. Visiting Aunt Lela was like escaping all my troubles and burdens. It was only three days, but it was three days of calm and security. As we drove back to El Paso, I felt I should share with her the experience of my feelings, the prayer, and the words of the voice I'd heard. She listened to me as we drove. When I was done speaking, she was silent for several minutes.

Then she looked at me and said, "Paul, we ain't much, but we're gettin' better, and it is up to you to help us get better. Remember how important you are to this family."

I don't remember much else that happened that weekend, but I will always remember her counsel.

I have sat with each of my children and most of my grandchildren and related this story to them. I have stressed the importance of the calling and responsibility God gave me that starry night. I tell them that the same charge comes to them by virtue of them being my children and grandchildren, that they each have the same direction and responsibility. I stress how important each of them is and that they are "key" to fulfilling this direction. Every so often, I remind them of my great-aunt Lela's loving counsel: "We ain't much, but we're gettin' better. And it's up to all of us to make us better!"

CHAPTER 5

The Strength of Samson

After returning to live with my father a second time, he started me working on the farm. This was just after Thanksgiving of 1969. Even though I had little experience working on a farm, it became my summer job. It wasn't easy operating farm equipment and doing the required chores with no experience. As might be expected, I created many mishaps and made many mistakes for which my father harshly punished me. As time went on, I came up with ways of fixing my mistakes before my father would find out about them.

My father was a man who could do just about anything with almost nothing. He also had a violent temper. He had made a deal with a man to earn part ownership of the farm and a small ranch.

We were extremely poor and had to jerry-rig almost everything. To make ends meet, when we didn't have enough batteries for all the vehicles and equipment, he would use his pickup truck battery to start the John Deere G tractor that I used to do the farmwork.

The G was a more powerful tractor my father had borrowed from my grandfather. Once the G tractor was started, my father would usually take the battery with him, leaving me with no way to restart the tractor if it died. There were many times I let that G tractor die and experienced the consequences.

Over time, I came up with a way of restarting the tractor. It was a simple solution that came to me one time when I was disking a for-ty-acre field covered in green tumbleweeds. My job was simple. I was to get on the G tractor, put it in gear, and start on the outside edge of the field, pulling a piece of equipment called a disk. All I had to do was drive around the un-disk edge of the field to the center until all the tumbleweeds were disked under. It was kind of like mowing a lawn. With such a simple task, I was left alone on the farm to ride the tractor. Everything was going great, and it couldn't have been easier except for the heat of the sun and the dusty air.

I had done about a third of the field when I began to feel a bump every once and a while. I looked around to figure out what it was but could see nothing. I decided the soil was just harder in the areas where I was feeling the bumps, so I kept going. I made two or three more rounds when suddenly, the tractor rose off the ground and stopped dead in place. I was high-centered with the back tires off the ground and spinning in the middle of a sandy flat field. How in the world could this be? I pulled the clutch and put the tractor in neutral. I climbed off and looked under the rear end and found a big rolled and compacted clump of green tumbleweed.

This was the monster clump of all tumbleweeds. I pulled out my pocketknife and hacked at it for a while with little effect. I got a shovel and tried to dig the soil out from under the clump, but it was too hard to get the shovel under the tractor and to the edge of the clump. In addition to that, I was making a big hole that my father could see, so I gave up the shovel idea and walked to the area of the homestead shack and the irrigation tank to see what I could find to help the situation.

There was a smaller John Deere B tractor stored in the area. It was an old tractor and too small for doing much work, and, of course, it didn't have a battery. At that time, both the pickup and the bigger tractor had a battery, so I walked back over to the bigger trac-tor and turned it off. I took the twelve-volt battery out and carried it across the field to the small tractor. I knew the small tractor had a six-volt electrical system and the big tractor had a twelve-volt system, but I decided to try it anyway.

I made sure the electrical systems of the small tractor were turned off except for the run switch. I checked out the fuel system to make sure it had gas to the carburetor. I made sure the tractor was in neutral. I then hooked up the battery to the cables, pulled the choke, and pushed the starter button. The starter whined as it turned the engine over and the tractor started. I pushed in the choke, jumped off the tractor, and disconnected the battery.

I found a twenty-foot-long chain, which I used to connect the two tractors. Then I put the twelve-volt battery back into the big tractor. I unhooked the disk from the big tractor, put it in neutral, and got off. Then I got on the little tractor, put it in gear, and pulled the big tractor off the monster clump of tumbleweed. Once off the clump, I rolled it out from in front of the disk and used the shovel to fill in the hole. I unhooked the tractors and parked the small tractor on the road next to the northeast fence. Then I got on the big tractor, backed it up to the disk, and hooked them together. I then pulled the disk over the area where the tractor had been high-centered.

When I was done, the only thing that gave a hint that I'd had any trouble was the big, compacted clump of green tumbleweeds in the middle of the field. I left the big tractor running in the middle of the field and took the small tractor back to the irrigation tank bank.

When my father returned, my work was done. I told him what had happened and how I'd solved the problem. He wasn't angry because my assigned work was done. Sometime later that summer, when it was all dried out, we burned the monster clump of tumbleweeds.

The small tractor had an electrical system that allowed it to be pull-started or run down a steep incline to start. During the summer, I worked on that tractor to keep it running. Most days with the G tractor running, I would run the small tractor down the tank bank, pop the clutch, and make sure it would start. When it didn't, I pulled it through open fields with the big tractor and worked on it until it started. Then I parked it at the very top of the irrigation tank bank.

The basic idea was to use the small tractor to pull-start the big tractor when it died. When the big tractor died, I walked up to the tank bank, ran the small tractor down the bank, popped the clutch, and got it started. I drove to a position in front of the big tractor and stopped. Then I ran the twenty-foot chain between the two tractors and put the big tractor in neutral.

Getting back on the small tractor, I started them both, moving at about five miles per hour through the open field. Once they were up to speed, I hopped off the small tractor, ran to the back of the big tractor, climbed on, put it in gear, and popped the clutch to start it.

Once the big tractor started, I put it back in neutral and hopped off. I would then run and catch up to the small tractor, climb on, and bring them both to a stop. The next step was to unchain them and return the small tractor to the top of the irrigation tank bank then finish the day's assigned work.

The system worked well, and I was quite pleased with myself. Then came the day when I rolled the small tractor down the tank bank, popped the clutch, and it didn't start. It just sputtered and rolled to a lifeless stop. I was at once filled with fear. My mind began to race. I walked back to the big tractor and tried to think of what to do.

I began to focus on the clutch drum, which was a shiny, smooth metal cylinder protruding from just behind the engine. The clutch drum usually had a guard to protect the operator from the spinning drum, but it had been removed. It was about twelve inches in diameter and about one-quarter-inch thick. I found that if I put the tractor in neutral and pushed in the clutch, the clutch drum could be used to turn over the engine. I played with it for a while. The problem was I couldn't turn it over fast enough to get the engine to start. I started to think of how it was a lot like a lawn mower.

I then went up to the homestead shack and took the clothesline cord down. With the cord in hand, I went back to the big tractor and wrapped the cord tightly around the clutch drum. I fashioned two shoulder straps, put them on, and took off on a run. It didn't work. I couldn't run fast enough. I then tried to use the cord just like a pull cord on a lawn mower. I pulled and jerked on the cord, but it just kept breaking until it was too short to use.

I started thinking again. If I could just wrap my arms around the clutch drum and pull them apart fast enough, it might start. I'd worked on the farm long enough that I was getting strong. I tried it a few times, but I wasn't strong enough to start the tractor.

It felt hopeless. I sat down, leaned back onto the tractor tire, and started to pray. The thought came to me that if I had the "strength of Samson," I could start the tractor. So I turned around facing the tire of the tractor and got on my knees.

I began to pray aloud. I asked God to give me the strength of Samson. I got up, wrapped my arms around the clutch drum once again, and with all my might, I jerked my arms apart in a rounding motion that would spin the clutch drum. The tractor coughed once, and there was silence.

I thought about why God didn't help me. I knew he loved me and didn't want me to suffer. I started thinking about what it would mean to have the strength of Samson. I thought I didn't need it all the time, just this once, and that I probably wasn't anywhere near worthy of such a gift. Besides, I didn't have the long hair that God required of Samson.

I got back down on my knees and began to pray again. This time, I told God that I knew I wasn't worthy of such a gift and that I didn't have the hair that God had required of Samson. But I did need his help. I promised God that I would live more faithfully and keep the commandments better. I told God I loved Him and really wanted to be a better boy and that I desperately needed this gift this one time. I closed my prayer in the name of Jesus Christ.

I got up. I felt so powerful, so strong. I wrapped my arms around the clutch drum again. I closed my eyes and began to squeeze with all my might. I could feel the cylinder bowing and deforming in my arms like it was about to be crushed. In my mind, I could see a finger on the trigger of a gun. I thought to myself, *When the gun goes off, I'll jerk my arms apart with all my might.*

I waited. I was ready. With my eyes closed, I heard the click of a trigger and saw a flash of smoke. With everything I had, I jerked my arms apart in a rounding motion, which spun the clutch drum. The tractor roared to life, and black smoke rose from the exhaust.

It started. I was so happy! I stood there and thanked God over and over again.

After regaining my composure, I saw that there was a three-inch patch of skin hanging from the palm of my left hand. It kind of looked like splintered wood, and it went into my palm about a half inch. It wasn't bleeding badly, so I found axle grease and an old rag. I applied the grease and wrapped my hand in the rag. I then climbed up onto the big tractor and finished my work.

That night, I showed my father my hand and told him what had happened. He said I was silly to be saying and doing such things. But when I show my children and grandchildren the one-half-inch scar in the center of the palm of my left hand and when I bear witness to God, his love for all of us, and how he answers prayers and gives us mighty gifts when needed, it isn't silly.

CHAPTER 6

Promises for a Lifetime

It was just over three weeks since the big row with my father. It had taken every moment of that time to heal to the point where I could move without pain. All the while, I was working up the courage and determination to run away the next time there was the slightest chance my father could get angry with me again.

As with many things, the whole incident started over a small comment. We were laying an aluminum main irrigation pipe run from the pump to the lower end of the farm then to a forty-acre plot where we were preparing to grow milo grain. I thought I could show him how we could do the job better and more quickly. But he took my comment to mean I thought he wasn't smart enough to figure out the problem on his own.

He flew into a rage, grabbed a fifteen-inch crescent wrench, and came after me. I stumbled to my feet and I ran into the open field I'd just finished disking a few days before. I looked back and saw he'd stopped chasing me on foot and was going back for the pickup. Knowing it would be easier for him to catch me with the pickup in an open flat field, I turned and ran toward the rowed-up field where we were going to plant the milo.

I jumped the ditch, which was about three feet deep and six feet across. I ran a short distance into the field. I thought I was out of reach there on the other side of the irrigation ditch; I was wrong.

I looked back just in time to see him jump the pickup over the ditch and into the rowed-up field.

I turned and ran again. As I did, I said a short prayer for help. At that moment, I heard a voice tell me to stop, turn around, wait for him to get close to me, then, at the last possible moment, to jump to the right and inward toward the pickup so he couldn't open his door and hit me.

I listened to the voice. I stopped, waiting for the pickup to get closer. As it did, I edged a bit to the right side. At the very last moment, when the headlights were almost upon me, I dove at a for-ty-five-degree angle to the right, toward the pickup. I landed on my belly in the soft dry dirt.

It worked! He missed me!

Quickly, I rolled over and got to my feet as it started all over again. My father made at least ten runs at me. Each time, I faced the pickup and jumped out of the way at the very last moment. Once, during one of his runs, he hit my foot, flipping me around horizon-tally. I landed within one foot of the right-side back tire. I watched as it churned by, sending dirt flying into the air. Not too long after that, he tried to make too sharp of a turn and got the pickup stuck.

When I realized the pickup was stuck, I ran to a barbed-wire fence along the east side of the farm. When I got there, I stopped and looked back to see my father trying to dig the pickup out with a shovel.

I jumped the fence and started toward a windmill and a stand of cottonwood trees about three-quarters of a mile away. The dis-tance between was covered with stands of thorny mesquite, and it took forever to zigzag my way between them.

As I ran, I heard the pickup on the move again. I found a high spot, stopped, and looked to see where he was. He was at the south-east gate. I started to run again. It wasn't long before the pickup grew closer. It sounded like a train was coming.

When I stopped and looked back again, my father was driv-ing through and over the stands of mesquite. At times, the pickup became airborne, bobbing and bouncing, mesquite and dirt flying.

I thought that if I could get to the windmill and climb to the top, I could stay there until he cooled down.

I got to within about fifty yards of the windmill when the pickup passed me and stopped, cutting me off. I was exhausted and gave up. He started in on me. After the first few strikes, it didn't hurt anymore. I couldn't feel a thing. It was strange. I knew my father was hitting and kicking me, but the only thing I sensed was the sounds of muffled thuds like someone dropping a sack of beans.

The next thing I knew, he was yelling for me to get into the pickup. I tried several times but was knocked off balance as he kicked or hit me again. He finally stopped and grabbed me by the shirt and dragged me to the truck, opening the door and throwing me in. I could see the steering wheel coming at me but didn't have the strength to stop my head from smashing into it. I bounced and slumped into a ball on the floorboard and sat there sobbing.

About that time, my father got into the driver's seat and started yelling for me to sit up. When I didn't respond, he pounded on my back. Somehow, I found the strength in my legs to push myself up into the seat. I curled myself to the right with my head resting on the window and did all I could to control my sobs. It wasn't the pain of being hit and kicked that hurt. It was the pain of being so deeply degraded, of being the focus of so much disapproval, anger, and rage—of being so unloved.

As I sat there, I made the decision to run away. I knew it would take time before I could, but I vowed the next time I did something that would set him off, I would leave. I told my cousin Everett and my best friend, Rex, what had happened, and that I planned to run away.

Finally, the day came. It started out much like every other summer day. We lived about five miles from the farm. My father took me there before sunup. My assigned chores for the day were to cultivate the forty acres of milo, start ten rolls of siphon hoses, and move hand lines on the pasture grass.

My father promised me that if I had my chores done when he came back in the late afternoon, he'd bring me a box of 22 rifle shells so I could go rabbit hunting with Rex that night. I was excited at the prospect of going hunting and was working as fast and as hard as I could to get done.

For most of the summer, we'd been borrowing my grandfather's John Deere G tractor but had to return it. My father had somehow arranged the use of an Allis-Chalmers tractor for the work on the farm. It was low to the ground and orange with a long toolbar on the back.

I'd been cultivating the milo with the Allis-Chalmers tractor for about an hour and a half when I noticed I was running low on gas. When I got to the end of the row, I headed to the yard to fuel up. I pulled up to the three-hundred-gallon gas tank and put the last of the gas into the tractor. I was in a hurry, so I put the tractor in gear and pushed hard on the left brake. This whipped the tractor in place in a U-turn so that I could head directly back to the field.

As the tractor swung to the left, the long toolbar on the back caught the hose of the now empty three-hundred-gallon gas tank and sent it tumbling off its stand to the ground. I was horrified and scared to death. I moved the tractor out of the way, parked it, climbed off, and went to the tank. Because it was empty, I was able to roll it back over to the stand. The tank was about two to three feet in diameter and about four to five feet long. The stand held the bottom of the tank, where the hose connection was located about three or four feet high.

I was strong enough to move the stand around and set it back on its legs. I could roll the tank around and even stand it on its end. But even empty, the tank was much too heavy and cumbersome for me to pick up and put back onto the stand.

I was in a fix. I knew I had to either get the gas tank back up on that stand or head out. I tried several ideas to right the tank and stand. I tried laying the stand on its side and rolling the tank up to the stand with the hose connection outlet in the right place. Next, I got some old barbed wire and used it to tie the tank to the stand. Then I tilted the tank and stand upright using pry bars and blocks. I just couldn't get it high enough.

My next idea was to chain the top of the tank to the tractor with the tank tied to the stand with barbed wire then pull it upright. It didn't work. The tank and stand just slid along the ground. Finally, I tried to stake the legs of the stand in place so they wouldn't slide along the ground. With the legs staked, the tank and stand no longer slid, but the whole rig swung around one way or another.

It was clear that vertical lift was needed. So with the legs staked in place, I took a railroad tie and propped it up, leaning back toward the tank and stand. I then ran the chain over the top end of the railroad tie and hooked it to the top of the tank. I hooked the other end of the chain to the toolbar of the tractor and made several attempts to right the tank and stand with no success.

I knew that when my father returned, there would be nothing but trouble. I didn't want to face that. I didn't like the way I was living. But as bad as things were between me and my father, there were still other considerations.

Things were also not going well with my stepmother. We had very little to go around. I had two preteen sisters and a toddler brother, and just that week, my stepmother had found out she was pregnant again. I felt I was a real burden on the family. There was never enough food. The houses we lived in were never big enough, and I was often forced to sleep in outbuildings, shacks, and sometimes the porch.

My old bed didn't even have sheets or a pillowcase. All I had was an old green wool army blanket, a bare mattress, a pillow, and bed bugs. Every morning, I was covered in bites, and when I mentioned the bed bugs to my father and stepmother, they slapped me.

When it got really cold at night, I put several burlap feed sacks on top of my blanket. I was wearing worn-out, hand-me-down clothes and boots from my cousins. I was left to work all day from before sunup to well after sundown, and most days, I was fed nothing more than a liverwurst and onion sandwich.

The way things were for me, life just didn't seem worth living. As I sat there pondering the situation and reflecting on how miserable I was, I made the decision to leave. I walked to the migrant workers' shack to look for the things I would need. All I found was a water jug. It was one of those one-gallon thermos jugs that had Styrofoam around the outside with a carrying handle and a three-inch diameter lid. It was in decent shape, but the Styrofoam was completely gone.

I walked to the windmill that I'd tried to run to three weeks earlier. It was an extremely hot day already, and the cool water and the shade of the cottonwood trees were refreshing. I filled the water jug and checked for leaks. I was in luck—the jug held water.

At that moment, I was filled with a mix of fear, happiness, and excitement. I had concocted a plan in my mind to walk all the way to Kearns where my mother lived.

From having been given so little to eat, I'd learned to eat cacti and other desert plants. I figured I could find something to eat as I went. I knew there was a good chance I could die out there in the desert, but the more I thought about it, the more I decided I'd rather die than continue the way I'd been living.

I prayed to God. One of the cottonwood trees had a root that had grown up out of the ground about twenty inches and then turned back into the ground. It looked like a knee sticking out of the earth. I went to the tree, set my water jug down, and knelt in front of the root with my folded hands resting on its top. I closed my eyes and began my prayer.

It was at least a mile to Rex's home, so there was no one close enough to hear me. Speaking aloud, my closed eyes soon opened and turned toward the heavens. I told God how tough things had been and that I was running away. I told him I wanted to do better and that I wanted to go back to church. I told him I would rather die in the desert than continue to live the way I was living. I promised him that if he helped me get back to Kearns, I would always attend church. I would serve a mission, get an education, and marry in the temple. I ended my prayer and stood. Then I picked a point northward and began to walk.

It felt good to be free and heading back to that place that seemed more like home. As I walked through the desert, the sun beat down, and the temperature was over one hundred degrees and rising. I felt that sense of adventure and excitement that was always part of starting any journey. The first few miles seemed to fly by, and it wasn't long before I found myself at Interstate 10.

My first dilemma was where and how to cross the freeway without being seen and caught. Stuckey's Truck Stop was to the west, and I could see my grandparents' place to the southeast of my position. I thought of going to the truck stop and catching a ride with a trucker, but almost everyone there knew me. Surely, they would let my father and the authorities know they'd seen me and which way I'd gone.

I thought of Granny. I wanted to go to her, hug her, and tell her how much I loved her and would miss her, but it was just too risky.

I thought about waiting for a break in traffic and running across the freeway. It was probably the smart thing to do, but I was too afraid of being seen. As I got closer to the interstate, I saw six culverts coming out from beneath it and headed for them.

They looked to be about twenty-five to thirty inches in diameter. I figured I could easily crawl through one of them to the other side without being seen. What a great idea!

I looked into one of the culverts. It sure looked like a long way, and it grew dark in the middle. There was a big space in the median between the divided lanes of the freeway. After a nice long look into the culvert, it didn't seem like such a great idea. When you live in the desert, you learn to be aware of rattlesnakes, spiders, scorpions, and insects. Those culverts looked like the perfect place for critters on such a blistering day.

I reviewed my options again and decided that even though the culverts were dangerous, they offered the best chance of not being seen. But with six culverts to choose from, the only question was which one? I took a long look down each one. I even crawled a few feet into a couple of them and then back out again. It was tough choosing. So I folded my arms, bowed my head, and asked God which one I should crawl through and for his protection. I ended my prayer, made a choice, and began to crawl. I hadn't gone but a few feet when it just didn't feel right. I couldn't turn around, so I crawled backward out of the culvert. Once out, I prayed again.

The third culvert from the east side seemed right. I started crawling. It wasn't too bad for maybe the first fifteen feet, but then it became muddy with five to ten inches deep of cold, gooey, sticky clay mud. A few feet farther in, it became cool and dark, and there were spiderwebs. I hadn't thought of spiderwebs. They were everywhere.

When I was about halfway to the break between the lanes, my lower half was completely covered in mud, and my upper half was covered in spiderwebs. I felt crazy. I swatted anything that moved on or near me.

I stopped and cleaned the spiders and webs off me. I pasted mud over my bare arms, neck, and face. I then started to move through the culvert as fast as I could. It wasn't long before I was at the median of the freeway.

As I darted across the opening in the median, I heard a voice tell me, "Move to the culvert on your right." I did so, moving as fast as I could, swatting spiders when I saw or felt them. It seemed to take forever to get through, but I finally came out on the other side of the freeway.

What a relief—my head, arms, shoulders, and back were covered with spiderwebs, and the rest of me was covered in mud. I ran my hands over the spiderwebs to clean them off. They rolled into clumps that were thick in the middle and tapering toward the ends, kind of like two-sided tops. I wiped the mud off in handfuls and slung it onto the ground. With most of the heavy mud off, I sat in the opening of the culvert, looking out at my surroundings.

The scene before me held promise. There was a hillside sloping from the culvert to a flat area. The flat area was about fifty yards or more wide and ran between the freeway and a railroad track. Beyond the track, about a half-mile ahead, I saw a cattle-watering tank created by damming up the wash fed by the culverts. As I looked at the scene, I heard a train whistle blow in the distance to the east.

At that point, an idea came clear. I would wait for the train to get close, and just before it got to my position, I would dash down the hillside, across the flat area, and over the railroad tracks, using the train to hide my movements across open ground. I would be visible as I ran from the culverts to the tracks, but it would only be for a short time. Once over the tracks, I would run to the cattle-watering tank before the train passed.

It took some time for me to see the train clearly because the heat was coming off the ground in wavy fire-like flumes. This made even real objects appear as mirages. As I sat waiting for the train, it seemed to take forever.

While I waited, I scooped up small rocks and threw them at bottles or trash I could see from my position. After a while, I began to throw the rocks over my left shoulder into the culvert I had originally come through before moving to the one on my right in the medium.

Over the sound of the approaching train, I heard a rattlesnake. It seemed to be just behind me. I dove forward, lost my footing, and rolled down the hillside a few feet, ending up face down in the dirt and rocks. I scrambled back up the hillside, first on my hands and knees and then on my feet, grabbed my water jug, turned around, and dashed across the flat area and over the train tracks.

The train was still several hundred yards from the point where I'd planned to start my dash, but the snake had set things in motion, and there was no turning back. The train engineer blew the whistle several times as I crossed the tracks, but I kept running, not looking back until I got to the cattle-watering tank.

Reaching the tank, I heard the clanking the train wheels made as they rolled over the joints of the tracks. In a way, the sound was comforting, and the train seemed to be a safety barrier between me and the freeway and the trail behind.

The cattle-watering tank was a little muddy from cattle walking into it to water. I was still covered in mud, but most of had dried. My clothes and boots were stiff with mud, and my exposed skin was covered in dried mud as well. It was so uncomfortable that I decided to wade out into the muddy water in my clothes—boots and all—and wash myself down.

The morning sun had already raised the temperature to well over a hundred degrees, and the water was refreshing. I scrubbed my clothes and skin with cool water until the heavy mud was gone. I waded out of the water, found a dry spot, sat down with a stick, and cleaned the mud from my boots. Then I stood up, said a short prayer, and headed north toward Silver City.

As I walked, I saw a windmill far ahead of me, about five miles out. This was great luck. A supply of fresh water in the desert was the most important thing I would need to make it out alive. I quickened my pace. I studied the horizon and the flow of the land, looking for plants and animals, thinking about what I knew was edible, and coming up with ideas on how I could get some food. I finally decided not to search for any food until the next day. Sometimes, I just watched my feet step after step.

Sometimes, my feet stepped on a thin crust of soil, breaking the crust and sending up a puff of dust. At first, it was interesting to watch. Then it became hypnotizing. Step-by-step, the miles crawled by until finally, I found myself at the windmill.

This was a beautiful place. Cottonwood trees surrounded an old shack, which had no doors or windows but only openings where they had once been. The windmill was pumping water into a watering trough about the size of a bathtub. There was a pipe running from the top of the watering trough to an area thirty feet away where the cattle watered.

The pond had been there long enough to have a few willows growing around it. I was hot and dry, and that watering trough sure looked like a bathtub to me. I approached it and saw the trough was filled with a water plant. I found a stick and cleaned the plant out of the trough, letting the murky water clear.

I was alone in the middle of the desert, so I stripped down and took a cooling bath. It felt wonderful. In the heat, it didn't take long to dry off and get dressed. I filled my water jug and resumed my journey north again.

As I searched the horizon, I saw another windmill off in the distance, and I headed for it. It seemed that the route I'd chosen had a windmill every five to ten miles. This allowed me to have the water and refreshment I needed and still make good time. It also helped to have a point to set my sights on every few miles. As the afternoon grew late, I headed for another windmill.

Even from a far distance, I could see this windmill had no willows, trees, or any growth around it. There were no cattle nearby either, and it didn't appear the windmill was turning in the breeze.

I wondered if there was water there or if it had dried up. As I drew closer, I saw a small dirt tank. This had to be the smallest dirt tank I'd ever seen. It was about fifty feet long and thirty feet wide, and it was filled with water. But the water was murky and muddy. There were no cattle in sight, and there wasn't much more than a gentle breeze blowing. Why was the water muddy? It didn't make sense.

I walked past the dirt tank, set my water jug down, and looked at the motionless windmill. It had been shut down. The question was should I start it up and top off my mostly full water jug or move on in hopes of finding another source of water further on? I'd been lucky so far.

As I stood there, my eye caught something surfacing in the tank. I walked over to the tank and stared at the surface of the water. Was it some kind of insect? Maybe frogs, pollywogs, or fish? Was it edible?

I hadn't eaten since before sunup that morning, and it was getting to be about five or six o'clock. Something surfaced again. I kept close watch. Another surfaced and then another until I caught a glimpse of a fin and gray skin. They were small catfish! These were definitely edible.

It was at this moment that I woke up to the fact that I was in real danger. I had no matches, no pocketknife, and no way of catching the fish. And as always, I was hungry. I circled the tank, trying to think of a way to catch the catfish. I went to the windmill to see if I could find some wire to make a hook. There was plenty of wire, but I had no string or line to tie the hook to even if I could make a hook with my bare hands.

I considered digging the bank down and draining the tank. I found a mesquite stick and tried to dig at the bank, but the dirt was too hard and the stick too soft. I also didn't feel right about destroying the tank for a few fish.

I thought about wading out into the tank and trying to catch the catfish with my bare hands. They weren't very big, and they had very sharp stingers on their fins, so that was out. I went back to the windmill again and worked with baling wire, trying to make a hook.

Suddenly, a small plane flew overhead. I dashed for the closest mesquite bush, dove under it, curled up, and tried to remain still. Was it the border patrol, a rancher, or a search plane? I tried to get a good look, but it was turning dusk, and the plane was too far away to get a clear look.

Maybe they hadn't seen me, but I wasn't taking any chances. I decided to put distance between myself and the windmill, tank, catfish, and a possible meal. As I moved, I started thinking of how I would get food. I figured I was around fifteen miles south of Silver City. I wondered if I could find food or someone who would help me without turning me in to the authorities.

With the possibility of having been spotted, I decided I would walk through the night and hold up in a shady spot during the day. If I did that, I could get to Silver City by the following night. I probably had enough water to get me there, and with any luck, I would find another windmill.

There wasn't much moonlight after dark, and I could barely see where I was stepping. Off to the east, I saw the lights of cars on the Silver City highway. The highway was at least ten miles away. That sure was a lot closer than Silver City. I thought about walking to the highway and hitchhiking the rest of the way. Maybe a trucker would give me a ride and wouldn't turn me in to the authorities.

I stopped and knelt and prayed about what to do. I knew I was in real trouble. The next day was going to be a scorcher. I had no food and no way or time to get any. I only had about three-quarters of a gallon of water, and I had a feeling water would be scarcer ahead.

The city of rocks where my uncle had killed a cougar just two years ago was not that far. Coyotes were yelping in the distance. They probably weren't much of a threat, but I was alone in the middle of the desert, and they were a reminder of just how alone I was. I prayed for protection, telling God how scared and hungry I was and asking what I should do.

I got up off my knees and began to walk toward the highway in the distance. It felt right, so I kept going. As I walked, a voice said, "Go to the highway as fast as you can! Run, don't stop!"

I started running. I was bigger than most guys my age, about 5'11" and 190 pounds, and running wasn't one of my strengths. I didn't think I could run for long.

Now it had grown much later, and the stars and moon shone brightly. My eyes had adjusted, and I could now see the ground much better. I'd been running for some time when I realized I wasn't feeling tired or winded. I always got one of those side pains when running; I just hated it. But this time, it was different. There was no pain and hardly a heavy breath.

I looked around to see if I was really walking and just thinking I was running, but things were passing by quickly. I had to be running. I wasn't setting any speed records, but I was moving at a pretty good clip. Every time I thought about stopping or resting, the voice would repeat, "Go to the highway as fast as you can! Run, don't stop!"

I had been running and zigzagging between the mesquite bushes when suddenly I came upon a dark void in the ground in front of me. I stopped just in time. I was on the edge of a wash that looked a bit like a mini Grand Canyon—about twelve to sixteen feet wide, with no bottom in sight.

I lay down on my stomach to try to see the bottom. I couldn't. I searched around the ground for some rocks. I found four or five and dropped one over the edge of the wash. I listened carefully but couldn't hear the sound of the rock hitting bottom. It bounced off the sides of the wash before it ever hit the bottom. I tossed the remaining rocks out into the center of the wash. The thud they made when they landed sounded as if the wash were twenty or more feet deep.

There was just enough moonlight that I could see about six to eight feet of the opposite side. The banks were almost vertical. There was no way I could climb in or out. I ran several hundred yards to the south and then to the north looking for any way down and up again. It was the same both ways. I could follow the edge for miles and never find a way in or out of the wash.

The voice came again. "Go to the highway as fast as you can! Run, don't stop!"

The reality sank in that I would have to jump across the wash.

My first thought was *I can't jump, I'm too big and clumsy.*

My greatest fear is falling and heights. I thought I would never make it. I knew I would fall in and break bones and die here in the desert and that no one would ever find me.

The voice came again. "Go to the highway as fast as you can! Run, don't stop!"

I looked toward the highway. Way down south, I saw a car moving northward. I thought to myself that if I'd gotten this far, God would bless me to get over the wash. I knelt and spoke aloud, eyes open and looking into the starlit night. I told God of my fears and asked for courage and the strength to jump the wash.

I stood up, picked out a mesquite bush on the other side of the wash, and with both hands, I lobbed my water jug at it. It landed in the bush. I then went back about thirty yards and took off on a run toward the wash. I barely stopped in time and almost fell into the wash. I had chickened out! I was so scared, and all my fears rushed in front of me again.

I knelt again, and in tears of fear, I asked again for the strength and courage to jump the wash. As I got up from the prayer, the voice came again. "Go to the highway as fast as you can! Run, don't stop!"

I knew I had to do as I'd been directed. I knew the Lord would help me. I walked the thirty yards between the starting spot and the edge of the wash. I picked a spot about a foot back from the edge and marked it with the heel of my boot, fearing the edge would give way if I jumped too close to it. That would be the spot I'd jump from.

I returned to my starting point and took off on a run toward the wash. I focused my eyes on the opposite edge. As I got close to the mark, I shifted my eyes to it. My foot hit the mark. At that moment, I shifted my eyes back to the opposite side. At the same moment, I threw my arms up, and with every fiber of strength in my legs and body, I jumped.

As I sailed in midair, everything seemed to go into slow motion. I hit the opposite edge at waist height with my arms, head, and chest leaning on top of the opposite bank. From the moment I hit the bank, I began to claw and crawl my way to the top. The edge was sloughing off beneath me as I struggled upward.

Not hesitating, I kept clawing and crawling until I got hold of a clump of grass or brush and shot onto the firm ground in a standing position.

I was on the other side, heart pounding, breathing deep and rapid, bending over with hands resting on my thighs, and looking at the wash. I had made it!

I took a few minutes to regain my composure. Then I went over to the mesquite bush where I'd tossed my water jug and retrieved it. I checked it over. It wasn't leaking.

When I took off running again, it was the same as it was before the wash. I was running without getting tired, winded, or feeling any side pain. The feeling that I had to get to the highway as quickly as possible was pressing me onward.

I hadn't seen the lights of cars or trucks moving along the highway for some time. I was running in a near trance when I came upon a barbed-wire fence and had to stop quickly. I had made it to the highway!

I had no idea how long I'd been running or what time it was, for that matter, but I knew it had to be at least three hours, maybe longer with the jumping of the wash. I'd lost all track of time. I grabbed a post and jumped the fence in cartwheel fashion. I walked across the highway to the northbound side and found a comfortable spot behind a large mesquite bush near the road.

I drank the last of my water and threw the empty jug over the fence behind me. In the flat desert, one can see for miles. I saw the lights of two cars and an eighteen-wheel truck coming.

I thought to myself, *I'll wait for the two cars to pass and then get to the roadside and put my thumb out and try to hitch a ride with the eighteen-wheeler. Besides, I won't be able to tell if one of the cars is a sheriff or a highway patrol officer until they're right upon me, and then it'll be too late.*

The lights were still a ways off, so I prayed that I could get a ride all the way to Kearns. I checked again to see how close the cars and truck were. There was still time. I started to think of what I might say when I got a ride. They were getting closer now, so I got to my feet and stood behind the mesquite bush, watching.

Just before the cars got to my position, I found myself at the roadside with my right thumb in the air and my arm extended as far as I could. It was as if I'd been gently lifted up and pulled to the roadside by my right elbow. The first car sped by, and then shortly afterward, the second car flew past. I turned and watched them with a feeling of fleeting disappointment.

The truck was almost upon me now. Anticipation felled my heart. Surely, the trucker would stop and give me a ride. I stood as tall as I could, beneath my breath repeatedly begging the truck, "Please stop, please stop." The truck passed by me with a gush of wind. I watched it go, my heart broken.

There were no lights coming from the south. I felt alone again. I thought about retrieving the jug in case I came upon water while walking northward along the road. I even considered heading back out into the desert and not risking being caught.

As I stood there thinking of what to do, I noticed one of the cars had stopped a half-mile or so north of me. It was just sitting there. I watched it for a time. I wondered if I should walk or run to the car or just wait where I was. After a while, I became scared and thought about jumping the fence, running out into the desert, and hiding.

I became more concerned when the car turned around and came back toward me. I felt like running but instead stood there watching as it slowly passed me, heading south. The car drove for about two or three hundred yards, turned around again, and stopped on the side of the road.

I thought about how I must have looked. I was a mess. I had boots that my cousin Everett had given me. They were well-worn and turned my ankles and feet outward. I had on a horrible pair of pukey mustard yellow pants. My polo shirt was green with countless holes from battery acid. Topping off this vagabond attire was a very nice brown Bradley felt hat. I was ashamed to dress this way when I was working on a farm with the closest people a mile away. To be trying to catch a ride on a lonely road in the middle of the desert sometime after midnight was crazy.

After a while, the car moved toward me again, passed, drove another thirty yards, and stopped. I could see shadows and faint face outlines of people in the car looking at me. Then someone rolled down the passenger window, and a female voice shouted, "Do you need a ride?"

"Yes, I do," I replied.

There was a pause, and the voice shouted back, "Then come on and get in."

One of the back doors opened, and I ran to the car and climbed in. There were five people in the car. The driver was Dennis Stailey. Next to him was his wife, Sharon, and his sister, Shaunna. In the back seat was a young man named Doyle, and between Doyle and me was Dennis's other sister, Trisha.

"Where are you going?" Dennis asked.

"Kearns, Utah."

"Oh, really," he said, and things fell silent.

After a short while, Shaunna began to sing one of those silly campfire songs. She hadn't been singing for long when she stopped and turned to Trisha and said, "That was one of the songs we always sang in MIA."

MIA was the name of a teenage group at the same type of church I attended. Knowing we were of the same faith helped me to trust them and open up. Then came the questions as to why I was alone in the middle of the desert, hitchhiking. I told them I was on my way to live with my mother.

More questions followed, and it wasn't long before I was in tears and telling these complete strangers the whole story of living in shacks, going hungry, and the beatings and how I had just taken off that morning with nothing more than a jug of water and a prayer.

The group was heading back home to Cliff, a city about thirty miles northwest of Silver City, after seeing a concert in El Paso, Texas. I explained that I didn't want them to help me very much and that I appreciated the ride and food but didn't want to bother them any more than that.

It wasn't long before we were at Doyle's home. When we stopped, they all went in and left me alone in the car. It seemed to take forever. I began to feel very scared. I thought of getting out of the car and heading north. The ride had already been a great blessing. But before

I could, Dennis returned, and with a voice of authority, he told me I would be staying the night at his parents Bud and Nora Stailey's home.

I protested, but he assured me they would have it no other way. I didn't like the idea of imposing, but it felt good to know I was with these people. And as much as I didn't like this stranger telling me in no uncertain terms where I was staying and what I would be doing, a feeling of security and calm came with his words.

It wasn't long after Dennis had laid down the law to me that everyone but Doyle returned to the car. Dennis took us to his parents' home. It was dark, and I couldn't see much of the outside or yard as we went inside. It was plain that these weren't wealthy people. They were hardworking farmers, and this home reflected their industry.

Dennis's parents ushered me right into the kitchen where there was a hot meal ready for me. There are memorable meals in all our lives. This was one of my most memorable. It wasn't fancy. It was a goulash made with hamburger, macaroni, and tomatoes. But I'll never forget how good that food looked to me and how wonderful it tasted. The homemade bread and butter were the sweetest I have ever tasted.

As I sat devouring every morsel as only a famished teenager could, Brother Stailey called my mother and stepfather in Kearns. They had no knowledge of the problems and the horrible conditions or that I had run away and was trying to get back to Kearns.

When I lived with them, things were rocky, and I'd been far from perfect. I could tell that my stepfather was on the phone, and it was obvious from the conversation that my mother didn't want me to come back.

At that point, Brother Stailey got forceful and even made a threat that if they didn't listen to him and help me, he would bring me to Kearns himself, and it wouldn't be pleasant. I remember thinking my stepfather was a mild, peaceful, and small man who wouldn't fare well in a fight. I got the sense this man meant what he said, and I think my stepfather got the same feeling.

It was after that threat that things began to sound like my stepfather would not only allow me to come home but would help.

Brother Stailey told my stepfather he felt my life could be in jeopardy if I returned to Deming. After several calls between my stepfather, Brother Stailey, and the airline, it was decided I would take a flight out of the Silver City airport the next day.

Once the arrangements had been made, I felt more secure and relieved. Things were working out. Meanwhile, Sister Stailey had been finding clothes that would fit me. Being bigger than most of the men and boys in the Stailey family, I had no idea where she was able to find clothes at that early hour of the morning, but she did. They were simple: a clean shirt, a clean pair of brown denim jeans, clean socks, and freshly washed underwear.

I stood next to their washing machine and shared how I'd heard the voice tell me what to do in the desert and how I was only going to hitchhike from truckers and that I'd been lifted to hold my thumb out when their car passed me. Sister Stailey told me that Dennis said when they passed me, a feeling came over everyone in the car, and they were compelled to go back and help me. That they had stopped and discussed the feeling and their fears that I might be an illegal migrant worker or someone who might harm them. That they had decided to go on and leave me there, but every time they started, the feeling they should help me returned. They decided to turn around and take another look at me, stopping far enough away that they would be safe. After taking another look at me, they were still unsure, but the feeling that they should help remained. That was when they decided to ask if I needed a ride. If I'd been an illegal migrant worker or a hard-sounding guy, they would have driven off. But when I spoke, they could tell I was just a young teenager, so they took courage and offered me a ride.

The discussion led to a prayer of thanks to God for blessing me and allowing the Staileys to be part of that blessing. After the prayer, I was led to a bed. I think it was one of those fold-up beds you find in motels. I could still see the soft pillow, nicely made bed with sheets, and a tan fuzzy wool blanket. I could still imagine the fresh laundry smell when I think of the moment I crawled between the sheets. I stared at the ceiling and thanked my God for helping me.

It was about eight thirty in the morning when I awoke. I slipped on my clothes and went into the kitchen and dining area and then into the living room. I was alone in the house. I went outside where I found the family busy with chores and butchering a calf. They were very pleasant and seemed glad to see me. They told me that Sister Stailey had gone to pick up her mother and that the two of them would be returning soon.

Sister Stailey showed up shortly with her mother, Sister Donaldson. Sister Stailey introduced us and informed me that she and her mother would be taking me to the Grant County/Silver City airport. Sister Stailey and her mother then took me to the kitchen where she'd saved me breakfast. Not long after, it was time to go.

I went to each member of the family and expressed my appreciation for their care and help. Sister Stailey and her mother insisted I sit in the front passenger seat. What teenager would turn down shotgun? So with not too much protest, I agreed. Truth be known, I wished I could have stayed with the Staileys for a while. I hadn't spent but maybe twelve hours with them, but they were twelve wonderful hours, and I hadn't felt so secure in an awfully long time.

The trip back south to the airport was filled with questions and retelling of the accounts of what I'd experienced. As we drove along, I felt an overwhelming need to somehow repay these wonderful people. I expressed my appreciation and my desire to compensate and repay them for their help and expenses. They graciously told me that I owed them nothing and to not worry about it anymore.

I again expressed the need to somehow repay them. It was then that Sister Stailey said, "Okay, if you must repay us, help others who you come across in need of help. By helping others and being a witness of Christ, you will be repaying us."

I agreed and sat quietly for a time, thinking about the promises of a lifetime to God and the Staileys.

Before long, we were at the airport. As we pulled into the parking lot, the feeling of fear came swooping back. Without the encouragement of Sister Stailey and her mother, I couldn't have gotten out of the car.

As I walked into the ticketing area, things looked okay. The two ladies stood at the back of the terminal as I approached the ticket counter. I spoke to the attendant and identified myself. The ticket was waiting, just as my stepfather had agreed. I claimed the ticket and thanked the attendant.

Just as I turned to go to the boarding area, my heart and hopes fell. My father's youngest brother, Uncle Charlie, who didn't live far from the airport, walked into the ticketing area with a six-foot-five-inch deputy sheriff from Grant County.

The deputy asked my uncle if I was Paul Waldrop, and with his confirmation, he then asked me. When I said yes, he arrested me and put handcuffs on me then escorted me to his car. Sister Stailey and her mother followed. As I was walked to the police car, I could see that they were starting to board passengers onto the airplane.

Sister Stailey went over to those who were supervising the boarding and asked them to wait for me and that I would be boarding once we resolved things. While Sister Stailey was holding the plane, I told my uncle and the deputy that I didn't want to go back to live with my father. I told them that it was just too hard to live with him and that he hit me a lot. I told them that my mother had legal custody of me, and it was she and my stepfather who had sent me the ticket.

It was about this time in the discussion that Sister Donaldson stepped in, pushing me back and out of the way. She grabbed the deputy by the shirt and tie and pulled him to her. I was shocked but no more shocked than the deputy and my uncle.

The three of us passed a look between us. Here was this little five-foot-tall old lady grabbing a deputy who had seventeen inches and at least a hundred and fifty pounds on her. She looked him right in the eye and boldly said, "You listen to me, if you try to take this boy back, you will have to kill me first. Do you hear me?"

I was in awe! The deputy must have felt her resolve, as I did, because he decided to call the sheriff of Luna County who just so happened to be my uncle Bob, Everett's father. The deputy relayed the situation to Uncle Bob. There was a long silence. It was years later that I learned what was going on during that silence.

I'd told Everett about the incident where my father tried to run over me with his pickup, and in turn, he had told Uncle Bob and my grandfather. The three of them had gone over to the farm and windmill and looked at the tire tracks and my footprints. Uncle Bob knew what had been going on. He told me later he was thinking, *I should let him go.*

The silence was broken with the words "Let him go," and Uncle Charlie agreed, telling the deputy it would be for the best. I didn't think Uncle Bob even realized at that moment he'd even spoken the words aloud.

Uncle Charlie and his wife, Aunt Connie, had known things were bad for me, but they didn't realize just how bad they were until hearing what I told the deputy.

The deputy took off the handcuffs. I quickly hugged Sister Stailey and Sister Donaldson, told my uncle goodbye, and thanked the deputy. I ran up the boarding ramp as the attendants impatiently watched me, and the airplane door quickly closed behind me. I was directed to my seat. I buckled in, and the plane began to taxi. I could see the two ladies, my uncle, and the deputy watching the plane as we took off. Being airborne was a relief.

The flight took me to Phoenix, where I was to change planes for my flight to Salt Lake City. I watched the ground get farther and farther away. We were soon over open range and mountains. I looked around me at the people on the plane. A beautiful blonde girl was looking at me. She was about fifteen or sixteen years old. I was certain all eyes had been on me when the deputy had handcuffed me. I could just imagine what they were all thinking of me. I was embarrassed, but being embarrassed was better than the alternative.

The beautiful blonde girl kept looking at me and smiling. Of course, I couldn't help but smile back. It was one of those wonderful exchanges where not a word was spoken. It seemed neither of us was able to stop ourselves from looking at the other. Our glances were the only thing I remember of either of the flights. With her mesmerizing smile, it seemed we'd barely taken off when suddenly, we were on approach for landing.

The disembarking in Phoenix was just like any other until I entered the gate area. There were police officers at the gate. It was obvious they were looking for someone. I was afraid it was me. I very cautiously walked through the door into the waiting area. The police officers paid me no mind. They didn't even look at me. I just kept walking, trying not to be conspicuous, and went to the gate where my flight was soon to be boarding.

There were police officers there as well. I walked up, checked in, and boarded the plane. The officers didn't even look at me. I thought it was odd that I was on the run. I expected that they would come onto the plane and take me off. I wondered if my mother had changed her mind and wanted me returned to my father. I was sure she didn't really want me to return to Kearns and live with them.

The door closed, and the plane taxied and took off. I was going to make it! When my plane arrived in Salt Lake City, no one was there to meet me. With this turn of events, I was sure my mother wasn't expecting me to make it back.

I called home, but no one was there. *Maybe they were just late,* I thought. I waited for a while, long enough that even their running late couldn't be a factor. I thought about walking or hitchhiking to Kearns, but the idea didn't feel right.

I decided to call my friend, Rich. I didn't want to call him because we had gotten into trouble together in the past, and I wanted to stay away from any possibility of that. Still, I called him, and he said he would pick me up as quickly as he could. He showed up in about forty-five minutes. It was a great reunion. I caught him up on things while we drove back to Kearns. The feeling was indescribable as we pulled up in front of my mother's and stepfather's home.

I was afraid to go inside. It felt like I should knock or something. I went ahead and opened the door and went inside. At first, it seemed no one was home, but just as the thought came to mind, my mother yelled from her bedroom, "Who is that? Is that you, Paul? Well, you made it home."

She commanded me to sit on the couch. She started yelling and laying down the laws. She didn't even ask me how I was or what had happened to cause me to run away. As always, she kept going on and on. I felt angry and wanted to leave. She went on to tell me I was going to go to church whether I liked it or not.

I was furious. Not ten months before when I decided to live with my father because I wasn't getting along with her, I was sneaking out at night and getting into trouble with my friend, Rich; she went behind my back and made an agreement with my father that I wouldn't be allowed to go to church when I lived with him. She did this because she knew I wanted to go to church. I had been angry over her doing that for the entire ten months, and now she was yelling at me and telling me I was going to church whether I wanted to go or not.

She wouldn't let me get a word in edgewise. I felt like yelling back at her and telling her I wouldn't go, that I would do what I wanted to do. At the same time, I wanted her to know that I wanted to do what was right regardless of what she told me. I wanted her to respect me, listen to me, and understand me. That had never happened, and it wasn't going to happen this time or any time in my life. I wanted to share with her what had happened to me and all the wonderful blessings I'd experienced in the last two days, but as I sat listening to her, I thought she had no idea what I'd been through. In fact, she would never learn why I ran away.

As she yelled, I thought of the promises I made to God while in prayer just the day before, especially the promise that I would always attend church. I think if any boy could identify one act that was truly his first manly act, the next thing I did was mine.

I took several deep breaths, looked at my mother, and said, "You're right, Mama, I will go to church and not argue." It was hard to get the words out, but she stopped yelling and paused for a while.

Then she said, "Well, you had better."

"You can count on it," I replied.

I was sad that I couldn't share things with my mother. I have since discussed the events with my father, uncles, cousins, and Rex, my best friend in Deming, who I shared everything with. I have visited several times with the Staileys and have been uplifted by each visit. My children and grandchildren have heard this story many times and often request to hear it again.

Several years ago, I returned to the old windmill where I'd knelt in prayer. It had dried up, and the derrick was all that was left of the windmill. The watering tank was dry. The cottonwood trees were all dead. I found the knee-looking root, which was still sticking out of the ground. I kicked the dirt out from around it and broke it loose.

I kept that old dead piece of cottonwood root on the mantel in my family room. When I tell this story to my children and grandchildren, I set it where they can see it and show them how it was sticking out of the ground. Every so often, I glance at it and remember those two days in late July 1970 that I made "promises for a lifetime."

CHAPTER 7

Finding a Way

Rich and I had been friends since I was ten. He was two years older than me and seemed much smarter. Hanging out with Rich was my main escape from my mother. Any real trouble I ever got into was either with him or at his coaching. One of the reasons I returned to live with my father for the second time in November of 1969 was to prevent me from getting into trouble.

Ten months later, when I ran away and needed a ride home from the Salt Lake City airport, Rich was the one who gladly responded. In that short ride, we reconnected. This time, though, there was a big difference. This time, I decided not to do anything that violated the commandments.

Rich's family had lived a few houses down the block from our house, but while I was away, his father had died and his family moved two miles away. The distance helped keep us apart, but we still found ways to spend time together.

I started as a sophomore at Kearns High School that September. As the school year began, I was determined to keep the promise I'd made to God to get my education. I was made president of my seminary class and attended church meetings every Sunday. I joined the Navy Junior ROTC and the Red Cross Club and was enjoying school and church activities. Things seemed to be going well for a while, but it wasn't long before things at home went back to the way they were.

Living with my mother was like wearing a hundred-pound choke chain around my neck. My every breath was arduous, and it felt as if a dark, gray mist was over me anytime I was around her. Every idea, success, or triumph on my part had to be sabotaged or punished and her control and superiority reestablished. Every mistake or failure I made was exploited and heralded as proof of my inadequacy, unworthiness, and worthlessness. She didn't spare the rod, belt, or fist on any occasion. Life seemed dismal and hopeless.

The worse things got, the more time I spent with Rich and his family. I also found myself unable to concentrate on school… or anything else for that matter. As the New Year began, I found myself skipping classes with increasing frequency. Rich had already graduated from high school, and it became our practice to meet at his house and find a ride or hitchhike into downtown Salt Lake City. We hung around the mall and walked around, checking out anything of interest. If we had a little money, we would get nineteen-cent Dee's burgers. On several occasions, when we found ourselves without money, we asked merchants if we could do work for a set payment. It was easiest to earn money when it snowed, and the burgers we bought afterward were always a feast. It was obvious we were headed nowhere at a snail's pace.

Rich didn't know what to do with his life, and I couldn't live with either set of parents. Going to school under the current conditions was impossible. As much as I knew skipping school was inconsistent with my goals and dreams, it was the only escape from my troubles.

Sometime around the end of January, Rich and I hitchhiked to Temple Square. We found ourselves heading south down the east side of State Street in front of the federal building. Military recruiters had offices nearby, and they caught our eyes.

As a lark, Rich and I went into a couple of them. I had wanted to be a marine ever since I saw a Marine Corps band march in a parade in Derry, New Hampshire, as a young boy. The recruiters painted a grand picture for us and seemed particularly interested in Rich having already graduated from high school.

I asked if you could enlist without having graduated from high school and being only sixteen years old. To my excitement, I was told there was a way: I would have to wait to leave until I was seventeen, get my mother's permission, and pass an intelligence test. Rich and I could go in on the buddy plan, which meant we'd be kept together for boot camp, infantry training, and military police training. We would be together for at least nine months, and we figured we could do almost anything as a team. I was told that after we were assigned to permanent duty, I could finish high school and even get college credits. Enlisting now would also make us eligible for the GI Bill, which would help pay for college, and we could be enlisted for just two years under a program that had been developed as a way to avoid the draft. Even though I wasn't concerned about being drafted, the program was perfect for me because it meant I would be available to serve a mission as promised.

It all sounded good to me. I knew I wasn't ready to be completely on my own and support myself. I needed structure and discipline. The promises I had made to God, the Staileys, and myself weighed heavy on my heart. I knew skipping school wasn't helping me keep my promises.

The idea of spending the next three years living with my mother and trying to get through school and prepare to serve God loomed impossible. I'd spent a considerable amount of time trying to find a way to keep my promises, praying often, and asking for help. Despite my hopes, things grew worse and worse.

Enlisting in the Marine Corps was a great idea. First, it would get me away from my mother. It would provide me with room and board and skill training. I could earn my high school diploma, save money to serve God, earn college credit, and be honorably discharged—all by my nineteenth birthday.

If, by a miracle, I stayed in school living with my mother, the best I could do would be to squeak by with a diploma a month after my nineteenth birthday. I prayed with anticipation of confirmation of enlisting in the United States Marine Corps. From the very moment I walked into the recruiter's office, I had a feeling that this was the way of accomplishing the things I needed to do to keep my promises. The resulting confirmation from the Spirit only added to the hope I began to feel.

Now came the daunting task of asking my mother and getting her permission. I asked her, reciting every benefit of allowing me to enlist. Her answer was a resounding "No!" I was to get myself to school and buckle down and so on and so forth, blah, blah, blah. I didn't listen. I had known she was going to say no even before I asked. I even had the recruiter call her and ask her to let me enlist, but her answer remained unchanged. There were still several months before my seventeenth birthday, and I was determined to find a way to change her mind. I knew enlisting was the right thing to do, and I knew the Lord would provide a way, just as he always had.

A few weeks after she had lectured me about buckling down in school, I found myself skipping school again. This time, it was with a group of kids from school. On a whim, we jumped into a car that one of the kids had and headed out. Our first stop was for gas in Evanston, Wyoming. We talked, laughed, and discussed our hopes and dreams. I talked about going into the Marine Corps, serving a mission, and getting high school and college degrees.

Before long, we needed gas again. This stop was in Rawlings, Wyoming. We passed the plate between us to gather gas funds to continue our little road tour. After a quick check, however, we found that our eastward journey was at an end as we had just enough money to get back to Kearns.

We all got out to stretch our legs. While walking around the gas station, I saw a pay phone and heard a voice telling me to call my mother. I did. I held the phone to my ear and wondered what I should say. Then it came to me: I would call her collect and tell her I'd run away and would only come back if she let me enlist in the Marine Corps.

I dialed the operator, asked to make a collect call, and gave her the number and my name. I heard the telephone ringing, then the operator asked my mother if she would accept a collect call from Paul. My mother agreed, and we were connected.

Confused, she asked me why I was calling collect. With an arrogant, taunting voice, I said, "Hi, Mom." Again, she asked where

I was that I would have to call her collect. Encouraged by her confusion, and with the same voice, I replied, "I'm in Eastern Wyoming."

"What are you doing in Eastern Wyoming?" she asked.

"Why, Mother," I replied. "I've run away."

"But why?" she asked. "Where are you going?"

I said it was because she wouldn't let me enlist in the marines. Then I told her that if she wouldn't let me enlist, I might as well go somewhere that I wanted to go, like Arkansas, Louisiana, or maybe even New Zealand.

She informed me that she would have the police arrest me and bring me back. I told her that if she did that, I'd just run away again the first chance I got.

Then she said she'd have me put in a foster home. I responded with, "You mean you can't run away from a foster home?"

She trumped that with, "I will have you sent to Ogden to the state school, which is just the place for boys like you."

"Well, okay," I said. "But wouldn't it just be easier if you let me enlist in the Marine Corps, and wouldn't the Corps be better for me than the state school?"

There was a long silence. I waited for her reply. I could hear her breathing. She wasn't happy and was struggling for a way of getting me under control.

"Well, Mom," I added. "Do I keep going, or do I come back and enlist?"

"If it's going to be that way," she said, "you might as well come back and enlist."

I reaffirmed her comment by asking, "Then you'll sign and give your permission?"

She assured me she would, and I told her I'd be back at home that evening.

I had her agreement! In just over two months, I would be free. The very next day, I called the recruiter and informed him that I was ready to process the paperwork.

The next step was to take the intelligence test. With this test, there was no studying or preparation allowed. Not that I had any confidence that I could study and do well to begin with. I had failed just about every grade from second to tenth, the seventh grade twice. I was a sixteen-year-old with a third- or fourth-grade reading level. I had been called stupid, dumb, meathead, or other seemingly applicable label by parents, teachers, and friends alike so often I believed it. Let's face it. I'd done plenty to prove them right.

I wasn't looking forward to taking the test. It was a major hurdle for me. I must have prayed a hundred times every day leading up to the very moment I took the test. Finally, the scheduled day came. Rich and I caught a ride to the recruiter's office. We went inside, and the recruiter gave us instructions and set the two of us at different tables in the testing room.

The test was a timed series of multiple-choice questions. It wasn't at all what I expected. The questions they were asking were what different types of items were used for. Some questions were comparing one thing to another or asking what the differences between them were. Others were basic skills questions. I pored over each question as quickly as I could. Before I knew it, the recruiter informed us it was time to set our pencils down.

Rich and I were ushered to the waiting area to await the results. I was deeply worried. This seemed my only hope, and if anything could keep me from going into the Marine Corps at this point, it was failing this test.

If the past was any indication of the future, I had plenty to worry about. One recruiter came and took Rich back to go over his results. I watched them, unable to hear what they were saying. Time stood still. I wondered why they had come for Rich so soon and left me there alone. I thought to myself I must have failed and they were rechecking my test or coming up with a way of breaking the news to me that I couldn't enlist.

I was in a near panic when a recruiter approached me and said, "Would you please follow me, Mr. Waldrop?"

I'll never forget how strange it was to be addressed as Mr. Waldrop for the first time in my life. This recruiter was higher ranking than the recruiter I'd been working with, and that scared me even more. I could hardly breathe as he began to speak.

"Well, Mr. Waldrop," he asked me. "Would you like to go to OCS school?"

Without hesitation, I replied, "Sure, I would."

I knew that any schooling would help me. At the same time, the question shot through my mind, and I asked, "What is OCS School?"

"Officer Candidate School," the recruiter said. "Would you like to be an officer?"

Sheer confusion swept over me. Something was wrong. I replied that I was only sixteen and had quit school. He then asked me how much college I'd had.

"None," I replied.

He asked, "Have you taken even one semester or one class at one of the community colleges?"

"No, sir," I said. "I've only gone to a few months of my sophomore year at Kearns High School."

He looked at me with amazement and said, "That's too bad. With your test scores and even one quarter or class at college, you could be an officer."

I asked him what he meant. He said, "Mr. Waldrop, you scored extremely high on the test."

"What?" I said, confused. "That's impossible. I'm not very bright."

"That's not what your score shows," the recruiter replied.

Suddenly, it came to me that there had been a mistake. Somehow, they had mixed my test up with Rich's. I looked at him and said, "Oh, you must have my test mixed up with Rich's. He's finished high school and is very smart."

The recruiter replied by handing me the test and asking me, "Is this not your test?"

I thumbed through the pages of the test thoroughly confused. This was my messy handwriting. It had to be my test. I read through it several times to be sure. I looked at every page and every question. It was mine.

My mind raced. A lifetime of countless name-callings, labels, and putdowns came rushing back into my mind. I didn't want them to be true—part of me knew they weren't—but this time, I had proof that I could believe. With that truth, I now knew I could accomplish my goals and keep my promises. For the first time in my life, I knew I wasn't all that everyone had made me out to be. I fought to hide the tears that welled inside of me.

I handed the test back to the recruiter to process the paperwork. There was only one hurdle left to jump, and the only way to get over that one was to be patient and somehow survive until my seventeenth birthday. After all I'd been through, I figured it would be easygoing until the day came.

Not long after I passed the intelligence test, I went to the recruiter's office with my mother to sign the permission and enlistment papers. Usually, when my mother got involved with anything I did, I seemed to somehow come out on the short end of things, always embarrassed. Once in the office, she insisted that she speak to the recruiter alone. I was left sitting in the same waiting area where I'd awaited my test results. Just as before, it seemed to take forever, and I couldn't understand why they had to talk for such a long time.

When they finally returned, I was assured that my mother had signed the papers, giving the necessary permission, and it was now time for me to sign the enlistment agreement. A great sense of relief came over me as the enlistment papers were given to me to sign—but as I looked at the signature line, I heard a voice in my mind telling me to read every word of the agreement carefully.

I stopped and informed them both that I had to read the papers carefully before I signed. Immediately, my mother turned impatient, irritated, and pushy. I knew something was up. I actually felt afraid; I couldn't read very well, and there were several pages with very legal wording.

I read every word very carefully, rereading sentences I didn't understand. Everything seemed fine until I got to the number of years of commitment. It had been changed from two years to three years.

I turned to the recruiter. "What is this?" I asked. "I'm only going in for two years."

I was informed that my mother wanted me to be gone for at least three years, and the only way that she would sign was if they extended the enlistment commitment. I told them both that I had made a promise. That I had to be out of the Marine Corps when I was nineteen to serve a mission.

In anger, I turned to my mother and assured her that no matter what, I would not be her concern once I was eighteen. An argument ensued.

Finally, I said I would only sign the enlistment papers if I was committed to two years and that if they didn't change it back to two years, I was out of there and neither one of them would ever see me again.

I started for the door, and they both asked me to stop and agreed to change the enlistment commitment back to two years. The recruiter did so, and I signed.

Afterward, I spent most of my remaining time hanging out at Rich's. I did go to school on a few occasions, and mostly, I avoided being at home as much as I could while continuing to attend weekly church meetings.

About two or three weeks after signing the papers, my mother decided I needed to see a psychologist and set an appointment with Dr. Black in South Salt Lake City. After much argument, I agreed to go with her. I didn't see the purpose in it, but she demanded I go. Besides, I wasn't doing much else. There was no counting the number of times she'd dragged me to this doctor or counselor or that psychologist or psychiatrist. I had been drugged, poked, prodded, tested, and analyzed in every way they could come up with. No effort had been missed to try and figure out all the things that were wrong with me. Frankly, I didn't see how one more "shrink" could help or hurt, so I went. Besides, I thought it might even be entertaining.

We entered Dr. Black's office and sat down. He asked my mother what the problem was. That was all she needed. She went off for almost forty-five minutes straight. Before the doctor stopped her, she had covered every wrongdoing, misdeed, and stupid stunt I'd ever pulled off and even fabricated some. I was glad when the doctor stopped her. I had heard it all a million times and was tired of hearing it.

Dr. Black thanked her and assured her he had enough information. Then he told her that he needed time to visit with me alone. As she stood up to leave the room, my mother arrogantly turned and said to the doctor, "I hope you can help him."

By that point, I felt about one inch tall and mortified.

Dr. Black closed the door behind my mother and turned to me. "How do you feel, Paul?" he asked.

I told him, "Angry. Very angry."

"So," he said, "what are you going to do?"

I said, "I'm going into the Marine Corps in about six weeks, and frankly, I may never come back." I told him about my goals and promises of always going to church, serving God, getting an education, and marrying in the temple.

To my surprise, Dr. Black said, "That's good. You're going to be okay, Paul. Just follow through with your goals." With that, he stood up, shook my hand, and escorted me through the door.

The time Dr. Black and I spent alone was about five minutes. My mother's reaction to seeing us emerge so soon was priceless. She looked at the doctor and asked, "Is that all? That didn't take long!"

He assured her it had been long enough and that I was going to be okay. She tried asking several questions, but Dr. Black just kept reassuring her. It was great, and I felt good. On the way home, she tried to get me to tell her what went on after she left the room. I told her we just talked shortly and he ended the session.

Time trudged slowly along for the next four weeks. Every hour seemed to last forever. Finally, Rich and I went downtown for our physical exams. On a prearranged day, we went to a room with several other recruits and took the oath before a government official.

Most of our days before my seventeenth birthday were spent hanging out at Rich's mother's house or at his brother's house in Granger, killing time and waiting for the day to arrive. I went back to my house only if I needed to get clothes or something I thought I had to have.

About a week and a half before my birthday, I tried to sneak home to get more of my clothes. It was about 10:00 a.m. when I walked through the door. My mother heard the door open and came out of the hallway, yelling at me and telling me it was time I came home. She demanded that I clean the kitchen and do the dishes. I told her I hadn't been home for a week, that I would only be home for a few minutes, and she would have to do her own dishes. With that, she began pummeling me with her fists.

In the past, I'd crouched in a corner and taken the beatings or tried to escape. But on that day, I'd had enough. I grabbed my mother by the wrists, pushed her back against the wall, and pressed my knees against her legs with my toes on hers. She was trapped, unable to move.

I looked her in the eyes and said "You are not going to beat me anymore!" to which she began spewing threats, promising that when I let her go, she'd beat me within an inch of my life. "No you won't, Mother," I said. "You are not going to beat me anymore!"

"What are you going to do," she said, "beat me up?"

I replied, "No, Mother. I would never hit you. Despite everything, I love you and respect you more than that, but you are not going to beat me anymore."

With that, she told me that she would have my stepfather take care of me.

"He might," I said. "But you are not going to beat me anymore."

She threatened to call the police and have me arrested. I told her that she could, but that I was going to hold onto her until she promised to never hit me again. She agreed, and I let her go.

She went directly to the telephone and called the police. I sat watching her make the call and listened to her lecture me. I have no idea what she said. All I know was that it was one of those times when I seemed to float disconnected from my surroundings. I had conquered her, truly and fully. I had stood up to her without threats, without violence, and without anger. It was pure resolve and clear purpose. I felt independent, whole, and just.

When the police arrived, my mother told them she wanted me arrested. After they heard both sides of the story, they informed her they didn't have much to arrest me on. She asked the police what they could arrest me for, to which one of them replied, "Being incorrigible."

She demanded they arrest me for that, and despite their protestations that it was more than was called for, she continued to insist, so they took me in.

My arrest had to be one of the strangest they'd ever made. I was as happy to go to the detention center as if they were taking me out for ice cream. On the way there, I said that I'd enlisted in the Marine Corps and was due to leave in a week and a half. They nodded their heads and agreed it was a good thing.

I was taken to the youth detention center in Granger and escorted into a holding room with windows on three sides so that my every move could be observed. I had hoped to be processed right away but was told that wasn't going to happen. I was expecting to be moved and placed in a jail cell until going before the judge the next day.

I sat impatiently for several hours. I must have asked what was going to happen to me every ten minutes. After three or four hours, a nice lady showed up, and I was informed that I would be going with her to her home and family for the night there in Granger. She would then bring me back to appear before the judge the next morning.

I was astounded. There would be no jail. Instead, there was a comfortable home with a wonderfully kind family. To top that, they had venison stew and homemade bread for dinner and strawberry shortcake for dessert. Not only was I not spending the night in detention, but I was also having one of my favorite meals for dinner and my favorite dessert. There were just a few rules. I had to behave, I couldn't leave the home unless I was with her or her husband, and I had to go to bed at 10 p.m. and be ready for a court appearance at nine the next morning

Once I was settled with the host family, I called my recruiter and let him know what had taken place and that I had a court appearance the next morning. He said he would be there and would speak to the judge. Next, I called Rich to let him know what happened, and we agreed to hook up once I was released. I was to call him at his brother's home. With that, I watched television with the family, went to bed as scheduled, and was ready for my court appearance on time the next morning

The ride back to the juvenile court was pleasant. Once in the building, I was told to wait in the hall until called to appear before the judge. It wasn't long before I was escorted into the courtroom.

At the table on my right sat my mother, looking arrogantly triumphant. There were two people talking quietly at a table to my left. In the back of the room sat my recruiter, looking confident and encouraging me with his body language.

I was directed to sit at the table next to my mother. We were instructed to rise, and the judge came in and sat down. We were then instructed to be seated, and the judge spoke to the court. One of the people at the table on my left stood up and began informing the court about my case and recommended my release to my mother. The judge spoke quickly and slammed his gavel down, making a loud bang. I couldn't quite make out what he'd said, but the hearing was over.

I was released into my mother's custody. As we stood up, my mother in her regular, arrogant fashion turned to me and said, "I hope this taught you a lesson."

I looked at her and said, "It did, Mama."

I never told her that the lesson I learned was that I could stand up to her and protect myself without becoming what she was, that I had conquered her and didn't have to be ruled or demeaned by her any longer. I knew she thought I'd spent the night locked up in a cold, unfriendly system with unpleasant food and that she had once again subjugated me using the system. And I let her think just that.

The next week crept by. With just three days left before Rich and I were to board an airplane to San Diego, California, to report to the Marine Corps Recruiting Depot (MCRD), I decided to shave my head and have photos taken in one of those booths in the mall.

There were four pictures in a column, all black and white. In my black shirt, I looked like one bad dude. I looked scary. As a seventeen-year-old headed to Marine Corps boot camp in a few days, it was encouraging to see me looking so tough. I kept the pictures for several years until I realized I didn't want my children to see me looking so hard and decided to throw them away.

I went home on my birthday, packed what little I wanted to keep, and said goodbye. I remember hoping for a birthday present or a cake or something, but all I was met with was quiet tolerance for my presence. I know my mother was pleased to see me go.

On the morning of the twenty-seventh of April 1971, Rich and I boarded an airplane for the flight to San Diego. We were excited. We were heading for a real adventure, and we saw our future laid out before us with every possible promise life could offer to two young men.

We disembarked and found our way to the exit of the airport where we were to wait for the shuttle bus that would take us to the USMC Recruit Depot. As we stood waiting, we asked several other servicemen what we should be doing. One young officer ordered us to stand at parade rest until the shuttle bus arrived. We did so with a sharp "Yes, sir!" that I had learned in Navy Junior ROTC at Kearns High.

I often look back on that scene of Rich and I standing in our "civvies" (civilian clothes) at parade rest as ordered. Doing so helped me feel a sense of security. The young officer had to have ordered us to do so just for kicks. As others passed, they, too, got a chuckle at our expense. I must admit I chuckled to myself when I pictured us two boys standing in front of the San Diego airport, whispering to each other, asking if we really had to stand at parade rest, but being naive, inexperienced, and afraid, we couldn't do anything else.

CHAPTER 8

Moron on the Road

The few weeks before I started boot camp was an interesting time. Everyone who even remotely knew me had a comment or a tidbit of wisdom for me. I will always remember two conversations that had a profound effect on me. Mostly because I felt confused and hurt by both.

The first conversation was with my bishop who called me in to speak with him before I left. It was the first time I had visited with him since returning from New Mexico. He asked what my plans were. Excitedly, I shared with him all my plans for the next two years. I told him that while enlisted in the Marine Corps, I would finish high school and prepare to serve my mission. I told him I would be eligible for the GI Bill and that on my return from my mission, I would get a college degree. I told him of my promises to the Lord and to the Staileys. I explained how the Marine Corps would offer me the freedom I needed to accomplish all my dreams.

My bishop listened for a while before cutting me off. Then he began giving me advice. It was as if he hadn't heard a word I said. It was a strange and confusing conversation. He went on to tell me that I shouldn't worry about serving a mission or getting an education, that I simply wasn't the type to do such things. He said I would be lucky to make it through the Marine Corps or attend church. I left his office deflated, hurt, and angry.

The more I thought about it, the more I became certain my ever-critical, sabotaging, backstabbing mother had had a long talk with him first. That was probably why he'd called me in since he'd never done so before. The man didn't know me at all, and he had no idea of what I'd been through. I'd been gone from the congregation for most of the years between my eleventh and seventeenth birthdays. Mostly, he had my mother's words defining me. It would be hard for him to see me any other way.

To me, it was just one more person to prove wrong. And I was going to prove all the naysayers wrong.

The second conversation was with Rich. About two or three days before leaving for boot camp, we were alone in the basement of his mother's home discussing our plans and how the buddy plan was a great way for us to help each other get through the challenges that lay ahead for us.

Out of the blue, Rich said, "Paul, who do you think will leave the church or try smoking first? You or me? I bet you'll leave the church first."

I was dumbfounded that he would even think of such a thing concerning either of us. I asked, "What do you mean?"

Rich said, "You know, I bet you stop going to church and start smoking and drinking before I do."

I told him point-blank that it wouldn't be me and that I hoped he wouldn't leave the church either. After a short exchange about how we would stick together and encourage each other, we never spoke of the subject again. The whole conversation upset me. I remember wondering why Rich would say such things. Within three weeks, I would know why—and it would break my heart.

We boarded a plane from Salt Lake City to San Diego on Tuesday, April 27, 1971. Just over an hour later, Rich and I stood outside the San Diego airport at parade rest for most of an hour before the shuttle bus picked us up and took us to the MCRD. I remember the feeling of going through the gate. It was the first time I experienced any insecurity about going into the Marine Corps. Fortunately, I wasn't given much time to ponder that doubt. We were taken directly to the induction center where we were processed and issued military clothes. We then shipped our civvies home. It was a defined ending of a past life.

Next, we were taken for haircuts. The haircuts cost us fifty cents each, which was automatically deducted from our pay. It ticked me off. I'd shaved my head bald, and now the Marine Corps was going to give me a haircut and charge me fifty cents to boot. I protested, but there are no exceptions. All new recruits got a haircut, I was told, so I dutifully sat in the barber's chair as he ran clippers over my head as if I had a full head of hair.

One nice thing about induction was that we all arrived looking differently. There were all types of young men. Some looked clean-cut, some looked like hippies, some looked like street thugs, and others looked like rednecks—but within hours, we all looked the same. It was clearly the start of a new life, one with a clean slate upon which we could redefine ourselves.

For the first few days, we were part of a loose organization that was herded around picking up cigarette butts and cleaning the latrines and grounds. We were put on hold until there were enough recruits to make up a battalion, which required about 250 to 300 recruits.

We were housed in large modern barracks constructed of concrete and brick. After two or three days, we were moved to a small old WWII building that only housed twenty-four men. These buildings were called Quonset huts. They were about thirty or forty feet wide and fifty to sixty feet long. The exterior was covered in corrugated steel. Standing at one end, it looked like someone had cut a very large circle in half and placed it on the ground with one door and two windows on each end.

During this time, we were under the direction of a drill instructor. He was a big, gruff, crude man with a loud voice. It seemed he wanted nothing more than to demean and torture anyone who showed even the slightest amount of weakness. He would form us into crude ranks and march us to whatever destination, letting us know with every undisciplined step of his disgust with us.

He started us marching with "Let's go, pukes! Go! Go!" and would bring us to a halt, yelling, "Hippity-hop-flop-stop-mob!"

Then he spent the next several minutes yelling at us and telling us how sorry and what poor excuses we were for Marines Corps recruits.

Some of the recruits acted out, and he made them stand at attention and bark in their faces not a hair's width from their noses. If one was positioned just so, you could see the drill instructor's spit spraying the face of the recruit.

I avoided any personal attacks by doing everything I was told as quickly as I could, but I also knew my day would come, and it did. We were on a parade ground in formation, standing rigidly at attention. The drill instructor was busy yelling at one of the other recruits when a fly landed on my nose. I stood frozen as long as I could, and then when I thought he wasn't looking, I blew the fly off my nose.

The drill instructor saw this and ran to my position, barking and spitting, demeaning every possible aspect and attribute of my person, all within less than an inch of the end of my nose. It took everything I had to not start crying. Finally, I thought to myself that at least the fly was gone, and it became bearable. I was sure not reacting to his barking staved off future discipline.

We spent about a week in the old barracks. Sundays were different in several ways. We were not in structured training or commanded to clean things. We were allowed to attend church, handwash our uniforms, and we could write and receive letters. That first week was different as there was no real pressure, no physical training. We were assigned to a training company in the Second Battalion.

On our first Sunday there, Rich and I informed the drill instructor that we wanted to attend church. We were given instructions as to the location and time and allowed to walk there. We got there late just as a young marine recruit was being ordained. We entered as quietly as we could and sat in the back.

After the meeting, we went to the front and spoke with the leaders to clarify times and get instructions. I congratulated the young marine who had just been ordained. It was one of the quick, in-passing interchanges that was a formality. I also spoke with the young ladies who led the music. They were the only exposure we had to females, so they received attention from all the recruits attending church. I didn't know it at the time, but that meeting was not just any meeting.

The next day, we were moved into a bricked barracks and formed into a training company with platoons. Rich and I were placed in different squads, and it was the beginning of the end of our association. Rich quickly struck up a friendship with a recruit from Los Angeles. I think he was mesmerized by the guy's stories of fast and fancy cars, beautiful women, and parties. Rich seemed to distance himself more from me and draw closer to his new friend. It hurt, but I kept trying to connect with Rich to no avail. That very next week when it was time to go to church, I begged him to go with me, but he wasn't hearing it. He didn't go again during all of boot camp.

Now his question about which one of us would leave the church first made sense. I was heartbroken to my very core. Rich had been my only friend back in Kearns. We'd been friends since I was ten and he was twelve, through many a tough time for both of us. We'd promised to be there for each other through our journey in the marines, and now I was on my own. I wanted to cry, but a Marine Corps recruit couldn't risk being caught crying. The resulting torture would be too high a price to pay. I just kept the hurt in and continued to encourage Rich and kept trying to be his friend.

Boot camp was thirteen weeks long. If a recruit didn't perform well, he would be held back and had to redo that week until he performed acceptably. Every week, it was common for recruits to be busted back a week and leave the training company. It was also commonplace for recruits to join the company.

We also had several drill instructor changes. After two or three weeks, a new drill instructor was assigned to our company. He seemed as good as a drill instructor as one could get. I had heard he was religious, but, of course, no one knew for sure.

The first Sunday he was assigned, I became acutely aware that if he was religious, he was not giving me any breaks. He stood in front of the drill instructor's office and yelled at the top of his voice, "Give me my Moron on the road!"

His nickname for recruits of my faith was "Moron." He took me to the outside walkway and commanded me to "March yourself to church, Moron!"

I called cadence and sharply marched to church, at least until I was out of sight and earshot. Then I walked calmly to the meeting.

That same scene took place every Sunday from that point to graduation, and I enjoyed every moment of it. It saddened me that every Sunday after that first, I made the trek alone. However, once at the meeting, I was surrounded by faithful and kind people from both the community and the recruits. From week to week, looking forward to the Sacrament meetings gave me a sense of hope and renewal. Sadly, I was the only recruit out of nearly three hundred that attended church.

The daily routine of boot camp started at five thirty every morning and ended at nine thirty every night. Each day, we would receive training on military-related subjects. The only thing I remember from this time was physical training. We did what was called the "Daily Seven" at least four times a day, and then we ran for at least three miles. Every action was done in double time, from showering, shaving, and grooming to cleaning, scrubbing, and sanitizing. Precision was the standard such that the slightest speck of dust or wrinkle stood out like red on white brought down on the perpetrator the extreme wrath of the drill instructor who imposed upon him as much discipline and torture as one could bear.

On the eighth or ninth week, the entire company was bused to Camp Pendleton to the ensign shooting range for rifle training. Because I enjoyed hunting and guns, I looked forward to this part of boot camp. The command to pack our duffel bags and place our locks on them was given. We quickly went about our duty. All things seemed in order, at least until we arrived at the ensign range and were assigned to our barracks.

Somehow, Rich and I had both failed to follow the instructions correctly. One of the drill instructors let us know in no uncertain terms that we were in trouble and that later that evening, we would be disciplined accordingly. It was something about how we put locks on our duffel bags. To this day, I still have no idea what we did wrong, but I think it was just our turn to be tested and gauge our reactions.

It seemed strange that neither Rich nor I had any communication on the process; we just followed the drill instructor's directions, and somehow, the two of us were on the hook. I think they wanted to drive us even further apart, or maybe it was due to environmental factors we both shared that caused us to interpret the instructions the same way. Somehow, Rich and I, plus two other recruits, had incurred the drill instructor's wrath.

Later that evening, we were ordered to a position in front of the drill instructors' latrine. We were told to stand with our feet about three feet apart, then we were instructed to lean forward with hands together, thumbs touching tip to tip and our index fingers touching, such that the space between our hands formed a triangle. We were to place our hands on the floor in front of us, with our foreheads directly over the triangle so that our sweat would drop off our foreheads into the triangle area. We were to ensure there was a good seal between our hands and the floor. The four of us were left in that position until each of us had a pretty good puddle. The strain of holding such a position was exhausting.

After a time, the drill instructor came barking orders and took one of the other two recruits into the latrine and shut the door. The three of us exchanged glances as we listened to the rumbling and yelling coming from the latrine. It wasn't long before the door opened and the recruit flew out and onto the floor, the drill instructor barking orders to pick himself up and get to his duties.

I was the third one to be invited into the latrine. When the door slammed shut, the drill instructor grabbed me and threw me against the wall. He began yelling, telling me that I was going to learn to follow orders or I'd be lucky to make it through boot camp alive. He hit me with a closed fist on the left side of my face. Then he planted a fist in my stomach, punched me on the right side of the head, and gave me another to the gut for good measure. When he was done hitting me, he took me by the collar, opened the latrine door, and threw me out and onto the floor, all the while barking orders and shouting, "That will teach you to follow orders!"

The truth of it was his hits weren't very hard, and as I picked myself up off the floor, all I could think was, "Gee, my momma could have done better than that." Fortunately, I was smart enough not to say a word, or I'm sure he would have made a better impression the second time.

One would think that I'd have learned a lesson that evening and would stay as far from trouble as possible. No, not me! I was able to keep clear of trouble for a few days, but on the last day at the rifle range, the battalion was assembled with full gear, and we were to do a ten-mile forced march at double time.

Having been an outdoorsman all my life, I learned to always be fully aware of my surroundings. That day was no different. We were running in formation. I was in the fourth most-outside squad and was the second or third man from the front. The drill instructor was on the other side, calling cadence. Our company was the second in formation, and there were several companies behind us. The course was covered in tall dry grass that had been flattened by the company ahead of us.

As I glanced around, my eye caught movement in the grass below my feet. My time on the farm in Deming gave me immediate recognition; it was a rattler, and a big one. Without thinking, I plowed through the ranks and into the drill instructor, yelling "Rattler! Rattler! Rattler!" at the top of my lungs. My actions scattered the rest of my company and brought the whole forced march to a halt.

The company was ordered back into formation. All except for me. The drill instructor and battalion commander wanted to have a little visit with me. I had done it now!

In the interchange, I was directed to explain my actions. I told him about the large snake, that I was certain it was a venomous rattlesnake, and that I'd spent a great deal of time in the desert and knew them all too well. The drill instructors were ready to bust me back, but the battalion commander sent several of the other drill instructors from other companies back to search for the snake before any other companies marched over it.

I was deeply concerned that I had blown it and would be either set back a week or two or even busted out of the Corps altogether. At the same time, I knew I had seen the snake and that if I hadn't alerted everyone to it, the recruits could easily have suffered bites that would have made them extremely ill and possibly even killed them. I probably should have done it differently, but I was a seventeen-year-old kid. What could one expect? It seemed like forever as they searched for the snake. I worried, wondering what would happen if they didn't find it.

Eventually, one of the drill instructors returned with news that a large rattlesnake had been caught. It was concluded that my actions may well have saved someone from being bitten. They were amazed by how in all the grass I saw the snake. Truth be told, I had only seen about four inches of its length under my feet, but it was enough. I was just relieved that no one was hurt and that I was not going to be busted back or out of the Marine Corps. One other benefit of the rattlesnake incident was that the entire battalion didn't have to run the entire ten miles. Most of the other recruits were pleased and amazed that I didn't get into more trouble than I did over the incident.

The last weeks of boot camp were uneventful except for the final week. Starting on Sunday afternoon, we were assembled for a ten-mile run. The only difference was that every mile or so, we had to stop and do the Daily Seven. The first three or four miles weren't bad, but by the end, we could hardly keep moving, and, of course, we had disgusted and angered the drill instructor. So rather than returning us to the barracks, he ordered us into the workout pits, a large area filled with sand, and informed us that we would do the Daily Seven until we looked like real marines…after which we would finish the run.

He ordered us to start. At one point, as we did push-ups, I must have faltered because the drill instructor ran to me and started barking about how weak I must be and began calling me several superlatives. He topped this off by stomping on my right hand.

When he did that, my index finger collapsed as I fell forward. It was forced flat against my hand, overextending my knuckle. Pain shot through my whole arm, and I almost fell into the sand in pain.

Just at the moment I was about to collapse in pain, we were ordered to do a standing exercise, which allowed me to take the pressure off my throbbing hand. We were all tremendously fatigued. We had done numerous repetitions of the Daily Seven when several of the other recruits began to fall onto the sand, saying they couldn't do anymore or run any farther.

The drill instructor kept calling out exercises and the cadences, and we kept trying to keep up, but even more recruits fell onto the sand. I thought that maybe I should join them on the sand as the drill instructor kept going. More and more recruits gave up and slumped onto the sand. Now there was only me and two other recruits left on our feet, still attempting to follow the drill instructor's orders. Just as I was about to give up, he ordered us into the barracks to clean up.

I was very relieved. I went as quickly as I could to my bunk and tried to open my footlocker, but I was shaking so badly that I couldn't accurately turn the dial on my combination lock. The drill instructor was yelling at us to hurry, so I braced my shaking hands against the footlocker and was finally able to open the lock. After that, the drill instructor showed those of us who were able to keep at it a bit more respect.

Later that week, we had to pass the physical fitness tests. The two tests I was most concerned about were running three miles in less than twenty minutes and doing eight backhand chin-ups, especially with my injured hand. For better or for worse, I was blessed with an exceptionally long torso and somewhat short but large muscular legs suited for hiking uphill more than running or chinning up.

The day of the test came, and once again, I had done as much begging of the Lord as possible, praying that he would strengthen me enough to be able to perform the chin-ups, and somehow, I did just fine.

The run was last. I was sure I could run a fair distance, but it was the twenty minutes that concerned me. As I started to run, I began to play the song "Away from Home" in my head. I picked up the rhythm and slipped into a trance, playing the song over and over in my head. The next thing I knew, it was over. I had done it!

Throughout the course of boot camp, I'd used several songs to help me. Many of the things we were taught were not what a religious guy should aspire to be or act like, so on those occasions, I played Neil Diamond's "I Am…I Said," reminding myself that I was going to be what I wanted to be and should be, not what others thought I should be.

The day of graduation was a great day. Several of us recruits got together and reminisced over the past thirteen weeks. The training battalion had started with 287 recruits divided into three companies. Of the original 287 men, there were only twenty-one left on graduation day, and I was the youngest.

The graduation ceremony was just like in the movies: picture-perfect. Many of the recruits' families were in attendance. There was an assortment of officers in dress blues on a platform. We were all fitted with dress uniforms. We marched sharply in perfect formation, every move performed with exact precession to a position in front of the platform.

Graduation from Marine Corps boot camp is a moment of pride, honor, and accomplishment, and there is not one graduate that hasn't earned it by rising to all the challenges, conquering that inner fear and insecurity, and standing taller with shoulders back.

The feelings that rushed over me when the final anticipated moment was announced were nearly indescribable. As we stood at attention, awards and promotions were handed out. I don't remember a thing except for the moment it was announced and congratulations were extended to all of us having become marines. That moment was the first time any of us had been called a marine. In unity, we all exploded with joy, yelling and throwing our covers as high in the air as possible. We congratulated one another and enjoyed our shared accomplishment.

Afterward, we were allowed return to the barracks to retrieve our gear and take ten days of required leave. I was going back to Kearns to see my family and friends. I went alone when Rich decided to go with his new friend to Los Angles. I tried to coax him and all but begged him to return with me to Kearns to see his family, but the stories of parties, cool cars, and beautiful girls were too much of a draw for him.

It was nice to not be constantly surrounded by so many men and under the sharp surveillance of the drill instructors. Returning home was a strange experience. Everyone saw the same person I had been, but I saw the new person that only resembled the old me. For the first time in my life, home was not home but a place to visit. Having been totally sheltered from the outside world, it was surprising how fashions and fads had changed. I was also surprised how my view of people had changed. Having more self-confidence changed my reactions and perceptions. I was now a US marine!

Ten days of leave passed quickly. I had orders to report to infantry training at San Onofre Area, Camp Pendleton, California. The area was just southeast of San Clemente, California. I reported as ordered and was assigned to a training company. This time, we were all assigned a Quonset hut for the duration of the training. Many of the marines I was in boot camp with had also been in the same infantry training company as me, and it was good to be with them again. There were also others that we didn't know beforehand. I had expected Rich to be assigned to the same training company as me, but he wasn't.

Once again, it so happened that I was the only marine to attend church in my battalion. That first Sunday at San Onofre, I went to the area chapel a little early. It wasn't long before a young marine came through the door and introduced himself as Monty, the area group leader. It was comforting to have a kindred spirit to spend time with. As it was with attending church in boot camp, it was an encouraging and uplifting experience that strengthened me each week.

After that first Sunday Sacrament meeting, I was told Rich had been assigned to the training company next to the one where I was assigned. Infantry training was not as restrictive as boot camp, but there were times marines were required to remain in the assigned company area.

I put out the word that I wanted to visit with Rich, and it wasn't long before we met—he on his side of the assigned area dividing line and me on my side. He was a different Rich. He was glad he didn't go back to Kearns with me. He had thoroughly enjoyed the parties, fast cars, and so on. I invited him to go to church with me the next week. He didn't want to hear it and cut me off. Being so close, I thought that we could spend time on the weekends, but he had other plans. He now had a girlfriend in Los Angles and didn't have time.

I didn't know it then, but that was to be the last time I saw Rich for the next five years. There wasn't much of a friendship left. He had left the church and me behind. My heart was deeply broken. Rich had seemed like my only friend at times, and I valued him.

Infantry training was a lot more fun than boot camp. The obstacle course had live 30-caliber rounds flying over our heads although the exploding hand grenades and shells were just natural gas rigged to go off in proactive craters as we crawled by.

The barbed wire was real enough. We also got to fire every size weapon from an M16 to a 105 Holster. We also got to throw live hand grenades. We got to go on overnight bivouacs. All were very cool things to do, and I enjoyed every minute.

There were several incidents that took place during infantry training that I will never forget as long as I live. The first was the very much anticipated run up, over, and down something called the (foul-named) Mount, which was a small mountain on the base. Its full name was such that I can't even repeat it, but the name was well deserved. Running up the front side, one would think, *What's the big deal?* But after making the crest, it became all too apparent why it was so foully named. The back side was so steep that one could hardly stay upright. The steep back side was roughly three or four hundred yards down to a shallow dip, followed by a flat run of two hundred yards.

We all felt pretty good having made the run as well as we did. We rested for a short time, then it was time for the return trip. The sergeant gave the order to double-time at an even faster pace than before. We were all winded by the time we made the dip. The steep climb was so demanding that it seemed a miracle any of us made the top.

The sergeant halted us at the top and ordered us to turn around and account for every marine. Of course, there were several marines still at the bottom, so we were ordered to go back down and get those left behind. This time, when I got to the bottom, I grabbed one of the stragglers and all but dragged him to the top.

Once again at the top, the sergeant halted us, and, yes, this time, there were even more stragglers at the bottom. Again, we went back down the foul-named Mount. This time, I picked up two backpacks, slung one over each shoulder, and grabbed a marine with each arm. I decided then and there that we were not going back down and up a fourth time.

I'd had a couple of fights, as many marines do, and had gained a reputation for being tough. So when I began threatening to kick the daylights out of anyone who didn't help the stragglers to the top, the other marines listened. Now with three backpacks and two marines, I brought up the rear. I was so determined and angry that the last trip was easier than the first. I can't express how pleased I was to not have to make another trip!

The next incident that will stay with me forever was the gas chamber. Every marine was required to go into a Quonset hut filled with tear gas and stand there for an allotted time. The gas chamber was a couple of miles from our barracks. During training, we were issued a gas mask, and on the day of the gas chamber, we marched there double-time just before lunch.

When we arrived, half the company was ordered to don their gas masks and march into the chamber where we lined up in rows facing one another. Several sergeants and the company commander were there with us. One of the sergeants, who was not wearing a gas mask, pointed out several burning candles and told us that the fact they were lit showed there was breathable air in the room. At that point, we were directed to take a large breath, remove our gas masks, and hand them to the sergeant.

We were to not panic but stand calmly and breathe deeply. We were told that even though our eyes, nose, and lungs would burn, there would be no harm. All this made perfect sense, so each of us did as commanded.

During the instructions, a staff sergeant and the company commander stood in front of the door, observing the process. I was about in the middle of the chamber. The moment came when one of the sergeants came to me and directed me to take a large breath and remove my gas mask. We were all ordered to start breathing at the same time.

I took one breath and panicked. It felt like a sledgehammer had hit my lungs. I didn't think or hesitate. I turned and went straight for the door. I ran into the staff sergeant then into the company commander, taking them both with me as I exploded through the door—except I never stopped to open it. The door, hinges, and frame flew off the building and onto the ground.

There I stood, coughing and gagging, eyes and nose flowing, trying to get a clear breath. It wasn't long before several of the sergeants caught up to me and gave me one good scolding. I was marched back into the chamber where the door was held closed by two marines, preventing my exit. This time, I was able to stand calmly and breathe. I finished the exercise and was directed to leave the chamber and eat my lunch of C-rations.

I didn't know why I wasn't in worse trouble. In fact, it seemed to me they had enjoyed the incident and found it humorous. I'm certain that others had panicked and bolted in the past, but I think I may have been the first (or at least one of the few) to have plowed through the staff sergeant and company commander, destroying the gas chamber door and frame.

The one thing I do know about marines is that there is a certain respect for those that don't let anything stop them. I think if the door had stopped me, there would have been repercussions. Surprisingly, busting through and destroying the door may have been the one thing that kept me out of trouble.

Then there was the night the entire training battalion was issued twenty rounds each of tracer cartridges. Tracer cartridges are used at night and placed in magazines at every fifth or sixth round to let a shooter know where the rounds are hitting.

Each magazine holds twenty rounds. The battalion was marched to a location where several old vehicles were positioned about three to four hundred yards in front of a firing line. We were all ordered to lock and load, which meant putting the magazines into our weapons and loading a round into the chamber. The weapons were fully automatic M16s. We were then ordered to fire in three- to five-round bursts into the vehicles.

The display was amazing and awe-inspiring. I've seen only a few fireworks displays that were as remarkable as three hundred marines firing twenty tracer rounds each. That was the last night of infantry training. There was no graduation like there had been from boot camp—just an order to pack gear and report to a staging area to await orders to military occupation training.

It was then that I found out that, because of my age, I was not going to be trained as a military police officer as agreed when I signed up for the Corps. But now that Rich was no longer a part of my life, the agreement didn't seem all that important anyway.

CHAPTER 9

Lord, I Need a Friend

After graduating from infantry training, I was sent to a staging area near Oceanside, California. It was an area that was used to house marines returning from deployment or waiting for their next assignments. With no specific duties to perform, I was bored to tears, and the assignment lasted for weeks.

There were very few marines that I'd known in boot camp or infantry training. We played cards, shot pool, or boxed to pass the time. On weekends and evenings, we were allowed to go into town. The feeling of freedom was comforting. The experience of walking around with no specific place to go or activity to perform was new. Knowing that these conditions were to only last two or three weeks created a feeling of suspended animation with no accountability.

The days dragged along for what felt like an eternity. Then one day, without so much as a few hours' notice, thirty of us were ordered to pack our gear and board a bus. We were taken to Mainside Camp Pendleton, California, and assigned to the First Field Service Regiment, commonly referred to as the First FSR.

In the Marine Corps, everyone is given a nickname. My group of marines, thirty in all, were called the Dirty Thirty. I was nicknamed the Preacher, not because I preached or was always thumping the Bible, but because of the way I lived: I didn't smoke, drink, or participate in their parties. I had several standing offers from marines who would gladly cover the cost of introducing me to any and all vices, but I was committed to living the gospel and preparing to serve others.

One of the marines stationed in our barracks was a 240-pound, six-foot-four-inch redheaded guy rumored to have ridden with the Hell's Angels. His name was Dale, and he looked like someone had carved him out of a large block of redwood. He had a square head with curly red hair stacked on top of his chiseled shoulders, seemingly no neck. His bulging arms sported several tattoos, which only punctuated the general statement that this was the toughest man anyone had ever seen.

Before any of us knew him, we knew only a fool would mess with him. Dale showed up as we were stowing our gear and introduced himself, announcing to everyone listening that he'd be whipping every one of us new marines just to prove he could. Most of us decided to stay out of his way to avoid a fight, but Dale informed us that there was no way to avoid fighting him. He would find a way to goad every one of the Dirty Thirty into a fight.

Not long after arriving at Mainside, I struck up a friendship with a young marine who seemed to share values like my own. I found it refreshing not constantly being harassed or confronted with invitations to participate in inappropriate behavior. Then we had a conversation about certain beliefs, which deeply offended him and essentially ended our friendship.

That was a Monday. I remember it well because it had been three weeks since I'd received a permanent assignment to the First FSR. Adding those three weeks to the three weeks I'd been at the temporary staging area, it had been six weeks since I'd been to church.

I wanted to find out where to attend but had no idea where to begin, and the ending of that new friendship emphasized the fact I needed to act. I'd found a hill a distance from my barracks where I could pray aloud and was not likely to be heard by others, so I decided to pray and ask for help.

That night, at about 9:00 p.m., I walked up to the hill. It was a dome-shaped hill covered in grass. I liked it. It somehow reminded me of the tank bank I often prayed atop on the farm in New Mexico. I knelt, looked toward heaven, and began to pray aloud. I expressed my sorrow at not attending church and promised that I would do better. I explained that being alone and having no like-minded friends was hard and that many of my fellow marines were pressuring me to violate the commandments and my values.

I asked God to send me a friend. That I needed my friend to be an honest, faithful young man who would encourage and support me in living the gospel and who would need my support and encouragement as well. I told God I didn't know where to attend church but that I knew the meeting house was a good distance from Camp Pendleton. Because of this distance, I also asked God to bless me so that my new friend would have a car so we could go to church together. I then asked for the strength to be faithful and live the gospel. I asked for forgiveness for my shortcomings and mistakes and expressed my desire to be faithful.

On my way back to the barracks, I felt better and more determined to live the gospel. The barracks environments were usually noisy, irreverent, and crude. My prayer hill was a refuge from that world, and I always felt better after the visits.

The next day began like any other. At lunch, I went to the chow hall with everyone else. Mealtimes in the Marine Corps were an experience. The chow hall where I was assigned was rated the worst in the Marine Corps, but that didn't keep many from eating there. The lines were always long, and there were several groups that would let their buddies butt in line. These groups seemed angry and would love to have created conflict. Most of us usually said nothing and just waited patiently in line. On this particular day, the lines weren't long.

That chow hall served several regiments, and it was common to see the same people at the same time each day. After getting my tray of food, I looked around for familiar faces, but none could be seen. I was feeling close to the Spirit and noticed a young marine who I hadn't seen before. His head was bowed in prayer.

Those of us with religious inclinations always bow our heads and ask for a silent blessing on our meals. I remember thinking at the time that this young marine loved the Lord, so I went and sat across from him. He was still praying when I sat down, so I went ahead with mine. When I finished, I lifted my head and opened my eyes to a face that was vaguely familiar, but I didn't remember where I had seen him before.

The ensuing discussion led me to realize he had been the recruit who was ordained that first Sunday I attended church in boot camp. That Sunday was also his last at boot camp, so we'd only seen each other that one time before. His name was Leo. We visited as long as time allowed and then exchanged contact information. As Leo got up to leave, he turned back to me and asked if I was interested in attending a young adults' church activity that evening. I was excited and enthusiastically accepted.

"Great," he replied. "I have a car and can drive."

That afternoon was one of the longest of my life. I couldn't wait to get to know my new friend and attend the young adult activity. Leo arrived to pick me up in a full-sized bronze car. I got in, and we headed for Vista, California.

As we rode, I told Leo about my prayer the night before and that I believed he was the friend I had asked for. Leo agreed and told me that he hadn't been to the chow hall much because it was the worst food he'd eaten while in the Corps. He said he usually bought his lunch at the commissary, but that morning, he'd forgotten his wallet. When lunchtime came, he returned to his room to look for it. He searched everywhere and even tore his bunk apart, but it was nowhere to be found. Being famished, and as a last resort, he went to the chow hall where we met. After lunch, he returned to his room to find his wallet sitting on his dresser in plain sight.

Leo and I became more than friends. We became brothers. For the next several months, we spent every free moment together and were of great support for each other. Every Tuesday night, we attended the young adult activities, and on weekends, we went to any dance or church activity within a hundred miles. On Sundays, our goal was to find a family to fellowship with so we could feel the sweet Spirit of a faithful family. We would start out by attending church as far north as Laguna Beach and working our way south until we were invited to dinner.

Spending Sunday afternoons with a faithful family gave us peace and comfort, and it afforded us the opportunity to become acquainted with many wonderful people. On Sunday evenings, we found a fireside to attend, which usually featured a speaker who presented on some aspect of the gospel.

We couldn't count the number of times we set out to participate in a church activity with Leo's car near empty, but we somehow always managed to make the round trip and arrive back at Mainside without running out of gas. Leo and I met every evening we could and sat in his car, sang hymns, and prayed. We were family. Our favorite hymn was "I'll Go Were You Want Me to Go." To this day, it's still my favorite, and I cherish the memories every time I hear or sing it.

By the fourth month of my assignment to the First FSR, Dale, the rumored member of the Hell's Angels, had found a way to goad every one of the Dirty Thirty into a fight. Everyone except for me. He'd made short work of everyone he fought, and I was determined to avoid him. He was everything his reputation had led us all to believe. I wanted nothing to do with him, but I knew my time would come. Often, he claimed he was saving "the Preacher for last because he's the biggest and the baby."

My time finally came one night when I was assigned guard duty. I was to walk the barracks and grounds, making sure things were in order. This night was cold. I had just entered the barracks and was near my bunk on the second floor. I set my flashlight on my bunk and was visiting with the guys when Dale walked in and snatched it up. He loudly announced that this was his flashlight now. I, of course, protested that it was mine and asked him to give it back.

Dale's reply was perfect. "Well, if it's yours, then you'll have to take it back."

He had thrown down the gauntlet in front of all the other marines. He then turned and walked toward the other side of the barracks through the foyer. As I watched him go, a flood of thoughts ran through my head. The flashlight was a standard issue, and I could get a replacement easily. But I also knew Dale would find a way to goad me into a fight, if not this day, then another.

To not respond now would show fear and weakness to everyone. Not standing up to him would create more problems than getting beat up. So I decided to stand up to him and take my beating right then and there.

I walked to the center of the doorways between the two sides of the barracks. Standing tall and with as loud a voice as I could summon, I shouted, "Dale, that's my flashlight, and I'll take it back *now*!"

Dale began to swagger and boast about how he was going to have great fun whipping the Preacher.

As he came toward me, I continued to act as tough as I could. I took off my gloves, tossed them into my hard hat shell, and tossed that onto my bunk. I unbuttoned my shirt, took it off, and tossed it onto the bunk, trying to look as mean and tough as I could. I stood at the ready in my undershirt, trousers, and combat boots.

Dale came back into my half of the barracks and asked one of his buddies to hold the flashlight until he finished taking me down. He took off his shirt and handed it to the same guy holding the flashlight. Dale was all smiles as he raised the two clubs he wore as hands.

All I could think was that once he took his first swing, I would "be the windmill," hitting him as fast and often as I could so I wouldn't look bad in front of everyone watching. This was one fight nobody, including myself, expected me to win. All I could hope for was to survive with dignity.

Dale tried to get me to take the first swing, but I had a policy that I never started a fight. I told him that if he wanted to fight, he had to take the first swing. So he did. I anticipated his move and ducked to the left.

In my fearful state, I didn't realize that I'd backed up so close to my bunk. When he took his swing, his fist hit the bunk post squarely with a crushing blow.

As I ducked and moved, I rebounded forward with my windmill strategy. I hit him with a hard blow to the jaw. I followed that up with several jabs to the face. Suddenly, Dale was on the deck, moaning in pain. The entire fight lasted only a few seconds. No one was more surprised and confused than me. I stood there staring down at Dale as he lay on the deck with an injured hand, jaw, and sprained ankle.

He hadn't even tagged me once. It was over, and I wasn't hurt. After a long silence, almost all the marines watching began to cheer and pat me on the back. I could hardly believe it. I had fought Dale and survived. By lunchtime the next day, it seemed everybody had heard that a young marine nicknamed Preacher had taken down Dale in only a few seconds.

My nature was such that I never held a grudge. It wasn't long before I'd all but forgotten about the fight with Dale and moved on. Things seemed to be going great for the next few weeks until I went down to the enlisted men's lounge to play pool and relax.

I started a game with a marine I didn't recognize. When it was my turn, I leaned over the table to line up my shot. When I did, I happened to turn my head just enough to see the guy grab his pool stick like a baseball bat and swing it at the back of my head.

With no time to think, I simply sat down on the concrete floor, flipped a somersault, and jumped to my feet. He was at the end of his swing, and I grabbed him by the front collar and slammed him against the wall, then down against the pool table, and back against the wall. Finally, I shoved him onto the floor.

I asked who he was, and he said he was one of Dale's friends. As he got to his knees to stand back up, I told him not to come at me anymore, but he tightened his fist and took a swing at me. As he did, I kicked him squarely in the forehead and put him back down. I turned around and walked away. I went to the first sergeant and reported that I'd just been attacked by one of Dale's friends and that I left him lying on the floor.

Several weeks went by without further incidents. Then one night after Leo dropped me off from a young adult activity, I was walking up to my barracks when four guys came out of the dark and surrounded me. As they drew around me, I saw that two of them were Dale and his friend from the enlisted men's lounge. They walked in a large circle around so that I couldn't reach any one of them.

I realized that I was in over my head and began to yell as loudly as I could for help. Suddenly, the barracks door flew open, and my fellow marines poured out, all of them dressed in their skivvies. Each of them held a weapon, like a pick handle or shovel. They surrounded me, telling Dale and his friends to leave me alone and that if anyone hurt me again, there'd be hell to pay.

That was the last time I ever saw Dale or his friends again. Later, I learned that the first sergeant and company commander used the incident to court-martial and dishonorably discharge Dale and his friends.

CHAPTER 10

It's Jim

Not too long after my encounter with Dale and his gang, Leo informed me that he had been accepted for embassy duty training and would be leaving Camp Pendleton. The few weeks before Leo left was a tough time for me, anticipating the prospect of Leo being gone. I had no idea how I would get along. As has been my nature, I determined to just lower my head and move forward.

It had been two weeks since Leo left for embassy duty training. Even though I didn't have a car, I somehow found a way to attend a single's adult dance in El Cajon, California.

Being an outgoing person, I danced with several of the single ladies and was having a great time. But then I noticed a marine standing alone near the exit close to the restroom. He didn't look well at all, so I decided to keep an eye on him. Not long after I started keeping a watch on him, he made a dash for the bathroom. I quickly walked after him, and as I entered the restroom, I saw a puddle with numerous red capsules on the floor.

The marine was on his knees in front of a toilet bowl, hugging the porcelain and expelling the remaining contents of his stomach. I asked him if he was okay. He assured me that he would be fine. I asked him what the red capsules were. He said that they were drugs and he was trying to get high but had taken too many and got sick. I was shocked. I decided to stay with him for the rest of the night. His name was Jim.

Jim and I found a ride back to Camp Pendleton. When we got there, I invited Jim to go to church with me the next morning, but in spite of my near begging, he declined.

The next day, I attended all my meetings as had become my Sunday routine. Life in the Marine Corps was a challenge, to say the least. The work was pretty much like any job. My day started at 7:00 a.m. and ended at 4:00 p.m., with an hour for lunch. The challenge came in living almost twenty-four hours a day, seven days a week with every sort and type of man. There was constant bickering, loud intrusive music, and nearly everyone used the most base and crude language. Smoke filled the air, and inappropriate pictures of girlfriends and wives were taped to lockers and walls everywhere.

The enlisted men's club was just behind my barracks. Fights in and around the barracks were a regular thing, and the morning sun and breeze brought smells of rancid beer. Every night, whiffs of marijuana smoke would drift into the barracks.

The entire barracks was basically a central staircase with four locker rooms connected to big rooms that housed twenty to thirty men. There was no privacy.

Sundays for me were a day to feel and be filled with the Spirit. It was a day to associate with the wholesome church members and get a respite from all the crudity and perversion. It was a day I wished would never end. Going back to the barracks was like a transition from heaven to the drudges of hell.

The next morning after church, I visited Jim at his barracks. I found him resting on his bunk, still feeling ill from the night before. We talked for some time. We discussed how life was hard and hurtful and how many times there just seemed to be no hope, happiness, or joy. Jim told me that he sometimes didn't even want to live. He told me how drugs seemed to make things better, at least for a while. I felt his hopelessness; I had felt the exact same way many times. I knew those deep, lonely, lost feelings where you don't belong anywhere or to anybody. The only difference between us was that he turned to drugs and I turned to prayer and faith.

I told him I could relate to everything he was telling me and that my own experience was similar—that I was only seventeen and that joining the Marine Corps had only been to get away from the hell and abuse of my mother and father. I told Jim about how I'd run away after my father tried to kill me and how my mother was impossible and abusive.

He asked me how I dealt with it all. I told him that I'd turned to prayer and tried to live the gospel. Then I began to witness to him. That I knew God loves all of us. That I knew the Lord Jesus Christ lives and is our Savior. That Jesus Christ leads his church. That I knew having faith and living the gospel was our only hope. That our prayers are heard and answered. That when we turn to God, we will be blessed. That the Spirit will always strengthen and help us to face challenges.

I shared with Jim how I had been blessed with strength, direction, and peace when being abused, running away through the desert, and even joining the Marine Corps. I shared with him how I felt hope for a better future. I felt the Spirit and knew that he had it as well. I closed my witness in the name of our Savior. We decided to get together the next evening and visit again. We said our goodbyes, and I headed back to my barracks.

I felt great! It felt like I was walking on air as I went back to my barracks. I was sure Jim needed my friendship. I felt that I could help him, and I certainly needed a friend.

The next day seemed to drag on forever, but finally, the workday ended, and I changed into street clothes and went to Jim's barracks. I had no idea what we were going to do, but I figured we would come up with something—maybe hit the chow hall and go bowling or play pool. It really didn't matter to me. Spending time with a kindred soul was a valuable thing in the Marine Corps.

When I got to Jim's bunk, something was wrong. His bunk wasn't made. There was just a bare mattress and pillow. I asked the other marines where he was, and they told me that Jim and about half the unit had received orders that morning and were shipped out to Okinawa. He was gone, and I had no way of contacting him. I didn't even know his last name. All that could be done was to hope and pray he would be okay.

Over the next almost four years, I completed the remaining months of my enlistment and about twenty months of missionary service. With four months left of missionary service, I was sent to a new area that boasted a beautiful chapel, which the members had built themselves. It was much more ornate than any other chapel I had ever seen.

On my first Sunday there, the missionaries were asked to join a greeting line at the back of the chapel. The local church leaders were at the head of the line and close to the door. My companion and I were at the end of the line, and I was the last one in line.

As people entered the chapel, each of us would shake their hands and welcome them to the meeting. With the meeting about to start, I noticed a young man on crutches moving down the line. He had finally advanced to me.

Suddenly, he threw his crutches in the air, wrapped his arms around me, and with sobs said, "Paul, Paul, Paul!"

I was dumbfounded. I had no idea who this guy was although it was obvious he knew me. He pulled back enough to see the perplexed look on my face and realized I didn't recognize him.

"It's Jim!" he said.

Instantly, I was in tears. With the Sacrament meeting starting shortly, we had to keep our initial reunion brief, but we made arrangements to visit later that day. I could hardly wait to hear about the events of his life over the last several years.

I learned that Jim was currently serving as the secretary for the elders group. We sat on his floor and visited. He said that after he was transferred to Okinawa, he'd gone looking for a source for drugs but was unable to find any. He told me that he'd begun thinking about the things I'd told him and about the blessings and strength that came to me through prayer, faith, and living the gospel. Jim said he'd decided to find the church and started attending. He was now married and had a child. He was happy and had a testimony of his own.

I was grateful to have played a small part in helping Jim find the blessings and joy that come from living the gospel.

CHAPTER 11

Single Servicemen's Branch

Not long after I first met Jim and he was transferred to Okinawa, I met a marine named Terry. Terry was twenty-four and had two or three months left on a three-year enlistment. From the start, I was in awe of Terry. He was well-educated as a court reporter and much more mature than my other marine friends. It was from Terry that I'd learned that Dale and his gang who jumped me had been court-martialed out of the Corps.

At the time, Terry was working on the case, and when I told him my name, he recognized it. He had been a missionary just as I was hoping to become. He had even done his service in a foreign country. I must have asked him a million questions, especially about his missionary service. Terry was much of what I wanted to become. He was more a big brother than a friend.

One might expect that the seven-year age difference would create a distance, especially for Terry. I'm sure it was trying for him at times, but despite the challenges, we spent much of the next few months together. I supposed that having a friend who was trying to live the gospel was something Terry valued, even if I was just a kid.

Terry and I had great adventures together. We liked going to German restaurants regularly and attended special religious meetings. Terry taught me how to request and get what was called TDA or temporary duty assignment. When religious meetings and special congregational meetings occurred, I could request and get TDA to attend the meeting. Getting TDA meant I didn't have to use leave. For me and Terry, every six months, there were meetings called general conference which were scheduled for four to six hours on Saturdays and four hours on Sundays. For the April 1972 Conference, Terry and I requested TDA and were able to make the trip without using leave.

The time passed quickly, and Terry was discharged. It was not long after Terry left that the word went out to all the congregations near Camp Pendleton that a single servicemen's branch was being organized. Of course, I was all in and excited to belong to a congregation focused on the needs of those of us who were single and serving in the military.

Not belonging to any particular congregation, the servicemen attended whichever congregation appealed to them. The servicemen were often seen as untrustworthy interlopers, mostly because of the general reputation earned by those marines who frequented bars in town, got drunk, and caused all manner of trouble. But the new group changed everything. Suddenly, we were seen differently. We were good guys. It was wonderful!

The new leader was named Brother Lord. He was a great man and a serviceman himself, an officer in the Air Force, but he was only leader for a few months before he was transferred to Anchorage. We hated to see him go. He really cared about the group, and without him, it suddenly felt very small. Many servicemen who attended were also transferred around the same time, making the group even smaller.

Our new leader was Brother Rowe. One of Brother Rowe's first duties was to inform us that the branch might be disbanded because there were only two of us left. I was sick, but I couldn't let that happen! The group was too important; it was a wonderful blessing to us servicemen, and it just didn't feel right to disband the branch.

I asked Brother Rowe to give us time to see if we could find more servicemen to attend. I think he and the leadership were a bit surprised at the request—the fact was, there was a bit more begging than requesting—but in the end, they agreed to give us another month before disbanding the branch.

I didn't know what to do, but I did know that a blessing given to me told me that I would be able to influence those who may have lost their faith and that because of my words and the things I would do on their behalf, they would change their lives.

By this time, I'd been transferred from Mainside Camp Pendleton to the Chappo area. That Sunday night, I went to my new prayer hill in the foothills just north of my barracks and knelt in prayer. I told God that the branch was a great blessing in the lives of single servicemen. I told him that they were thinking of disbanding the group and we needed his help, that I knew there were many good servicemen on the base that were not attending church who really needed the blessing of being part of the group. I asked him to help me find them, and I pledged to do everything I could to get them to church. I ended my prayer, went back to my barracks, and went to sleep.

The next morning, when I went to the chow hall for breakfast, I was astounded. As the door closed behind me, I gazed out upon all the marines sitting at tables and standing in the chow lines. Several had glowing auras; I knew they were the ones I was seeking.

I got my breakfast and went to the closest individual with an aura. I wasted no time in introducing myself, talking about the branch, and insisting they come to the next activity. It wasn't long before our numbers had grown enough that disbanding was no longer a consideration. I must confess that I wouldn't take no for an answer.

Sometimes, I think, *Wow, how presumptuous and callous I was to push so hard.* On the other hand, I knew it was for the best. I loved the branch. Being a part of the group was one of the first times I felt like I belonged.

Brother Rowe was a retired marine, and he knew the system. On regular Sundays, the group would meet for a men's meeting at the Chappo area chapel. One of my assignments was to teach the lesson. After the priesthood meeting, all those in attendance would go to the chow hall and have breakfast before going to Sunday school at the Carlsbad congregation. Later, we all attended Sacrament at a chapel in an area just north of Mainside.

The group became my family, and I was the youngest. I will never forget twelve big tough marines sitting in a circle in Brother Rowe's home while Sister Rowe, who was from Hawaii, taught us how to make leis from fresh flowers. It was one of my most cherished memories.

For a time, I had very weak ankles while in the Marine Corps. I had never had problems before, but I could just be walking and I would twist my ankle and sprain it. It got to the point that they required me to have my right ankle in a cast for six weeks. I hated it. I loved to dance, bowl, and do all kinds of activities, all of which were curtailed while in the cast.

Finally, the day came that my lousy cast was to be removed—and just in time for a dance that very night in El Cajon. It was a Friday, and I couldn't be more excited to go, so I caught the base bus in plenty of time to get to the infirmary for my cast removal.

I showed up, signed in, and waited for what seemed forever. I finally asked what was taking so long and was told they were too busy to remove my cast. I would have to come back on Monday. I protested and pointed out that I had a scheduled appointment and I needed to have the cast removed today—at which point I was reminded that I was just a lance corporal and that I was to come back on Monday.

I was steaming as I hobbled back to my assigned area. With every step, I got angrier. I made the decision that I was going back to my barracks to take my cast off myself.

As I hobbled, I began to hit the curb with the cast to soften it up. Then I heard a Spirit that told me to "go over there and talk to that marine!"

"No!" I said. "I'm going to the barracks to take this thing off!"

But the Spirit spoke again. "Go over there and talk to that marine."

Again, I refused, and again, the Spirit urged me on. Finally, I said, "Okay, but then I'm going back to the barracks to take this thing off."

There was a marine about fifty yards away putting computer cards into a dumpster. When he turned to go back toward his office, I called out to him. "Wait! I need to talk to you."

The marine just quickened his step, and with my cast, I couldn't match his speed.

"Please, wait!" I said. "I need to talk to you."

He got to his office door and kindly waited a moment. I caught up to him and just stood there, to which he said "Yeah?" with a harshness in his tone.

It was at that moment that I realized I had no idea what to say to this marine. I stood staring at him for another moment when the Spirit spoke again. "He is from Utah," the Spirit told me.

"You're from Utah," I said.

"Yeah," he replied.

I stood there for another moment, again not knowing what to say when the Spirit said to me, "He is from American Fork."

I repeated the words and the marine replied "Yeah," but this time, his voice was softer.

The Spirit then told me he was a member of the church.

"You're a member of the church," I said.

He replied "Yeah" with more tender tones and a look of amazement forming on his face.

"He was ordained six months ago," the Spirit told me. "And he has not been to church since."

I repeated this to the marine, and again, he replied, "Yeah."

At this point, I didn't need the Spirit to tell me what to say anymore. I looked at the marine and asked him, "Will you go to church with me this week?"

"No," he replied, "but I'll go with you next week."

As it turned out, he kept his promise, and he eventually became our servicemen's group leader and a dear friend. The branch went on for years, blessing the lives of numerous single servicemen. I was honored to be the first full-time missionary to be called from the branch. I was discharged at the end of April 1973. Leaving the branch family was one of the toughest things I ever did.

CHAPTER 12

So You're Going on a Mission

While in the Marine Corps, I had one overriding goal. That was to prepare and serve in a mission. But first, I had to fulfill the first requirement: to have a high school diploma or pass the GED exam. As soon as I had served six months, I became eligible to take the GED, so with much trepidation, I arranged to take it. I fully expected to do poorly, but I had to try. I had to find a way to keep the promises I had made to God, the Staileys, and myself. I had pretty much failed every year of school from third grade to tenth grade, of which I only attended maybe three months before dropping out of school altogether. In today's world, I'm sure I would have been diagnosed with dyslexia as well as the ADD I was diagnosed with at eleven.

As I sat in the exam location waiting room, I begged God to somehow bless me to do well. Taking a written test that I had to read and comprehend was one of those things I feared the most. Reading had always been an extremely tough subject for me, and I made little progress even when being tutored three times a week.

I remember vividly my sixth-grade tutor endlessly having me repeat my vowels and her frustration with my never getting them correct. She would say "A-E-I-O-U and sometimes Y," and I would repeat exactly what she said. Then she'd roll her eyes in frustration and ask me to try again. Now that I understand dyslexia, I'm sure I was trying but failing to repeat her exactly as she expected.

I never got the spelling, vowels, nouns, or grammar things, and I still struggle to this day. Most of the time, everything seemed mixed up to me. I seemed to do much better at math, depending on the teacher. When I was seven and living in Almo, Idaho, I advanced to the third grade from the first grade and did well for a while, but when my family moved to Kearns and I was enrolled in David Gourley Elementary, I was forced back to the second grade. From that point on, it seemed I did increasingly poorly. I was in and out of no less than ten schools, constantly in some sort of trouble, and, of course, things at home with my mother were always abusive, demeaning, and depressing.

At the time, taking the GED exam was one of the greatest hurdles in my life, but I stood up straight, and, repeating my begging prayer, I went in and did my best. I read and reread every question as fast as I could. When the test was over and I hadn't completed all the questions, I was certain I had failed even though afterward the administrator told me I could still pass even if I didn't complete the test.

It was several weeks before the results came back. To my surprise, I passed—and not only did I pass, but I also scored high enough in several subject areas to qualify for a special program. In this program, the Army-Navy Academy, a local accredited private military high school in Carlsbad, would award me a high school diploma if I completed several night classes. With an actual high school diploma within reach, I had to take advantage of the opportunity, and I did.

By the end of 1972, I had finished all the night classes. Back in Utah, I had been held back, but now here I finished the requirements for a diploma the very same year I should have graduated. My high school diploma came in January 1973.

I had started out with no idea how I was going to keep the promises I had made, but God provided a way. I could proudly apply to serve and honestly state I had a high school diploma. I was also eligible to attend college, which was yet another one of my promises.

Just after I finished the coursework at the Army-Navy Academy and still with over six months left of my enlistment, I was to have one last fight: one that would change my life in a way I could have never expected.

I was assigned KP (kitchen patrol) duty for two weeks. It was a fun break from the usual duties. Things were going well until for some unknown reason, one of the other marines became upset with me. He was a big guy, even bigger than me. I tried to resolve the issue, but he was intent on conflict and a fight.

At one point, he said to me, "I've heard of you, but I don't believe it."

I asked him what he meant, and he told me that I had a reputation for being tough but that I didn't seem all that tough to him. And he wanted to prove it by kicking my behind. I told him I didn't have anything to prove, but he just kept insulting and challenging me in front of the other marines.

Loudly, he proclaimed that I was nothing more than an eighteen-year-old punk. I became so embarrassed and humiliated that I finally agreed to fight him.

I followed him outside in back of the chow hall kitchen. We were both dressed in our white KP uniforms. We put our fists up, and he took a swing at me. I dodged it and sent a blow to the left side of his face. I followed that with two more quick jabs that connected with his nose and mouth. With only three punches, the guy had a black eye and a bloody nose and lip. At that point, I called the fight and told him he was whipped. I walked back to the KP locker room to change my uniform, which was now covered in his blood.

I was sitting on a bench removing my boots when the guy approached me again and demanded that I come back and finish the fight. I pointed out that I'd already beat him and I wasn't going to fight anymore.

He left, but after just a few minutes, he came back with a gunnery sergeant (gunny). This particular gunny disliked me, and he ordered me to resume the fight. I put my boots back on and did what I was told. We went back outside, and immediately, the marine came at me.

One thing about me, I was what's called a switch hitter. This meant I could lead with fists in either a right-handed or left-handed stance. So I did just that. I switched hands, and in short order, I had blackened the marine's other eye and bloodied the other side of his nose and lips.

The guy was now little more than a bloody mess, so I dropped my fists and started to back away. As I did, he landed a heavy blow to the center of my forehead. I started to walk away. I told him that if he wasn't whipped before, he was certainly whipped now, and I was ending the fight, but he and the gunny both demanded the fight continue.

I indulged them, mostly now just blocking and dodging the guy's punches until it finally grew tiresome and irritating. The guy was no match for me, and he was getting hurt. I took a step back and said I didn't want to fight anymore and that if it continued, I'd wind up sending him to the hospital. But the fool simply laughed and came at me again.

This time, I unloaded everything I had. I hit and kicked him repeatedly with such fury that eventually the only thing keeping him upright were my punches and kicks. Once again, I stopped and backed off. This time, the marine fell to the ground and lay still. Bystanders checked him to see if he was breathing. To my relief, he was, so they called for an ambulance and took him to the hospital. I went back into the locker room, changed my uniform, and resumed my KP duties.

The battalion investigated the fight, but because I had only been defending myself and following the gunny's orders, I wasn't charged with any violations. Later, I heard that even the gunny got into trouble for his actions.

Three or four days later, the same marine showed up at the chow hall in a wheelchair. He was a red-, yellow-, black-, and blue-bruised mess from his head to toes. Oddly, he didn't seem upset that he was hurt. He laughed and seemed pleased over the whole incident, which led me to conclude that he was one of those people who actually enjoyed being hurt.

Regardless of how he felt, I felt sick, deeply ashamed, and sad. I had to learn to fight to survive, and it served me well. But this time, I realized I'd let things go too far. I had really hurt someone who wasn't even a threat to me. It was nothing more than childish pride that had led me to fight. This was not okay or justified. Here I was, planning to serve others and teach about Jesus Christ, and I had just horribly beaten one of God's children nearly to death.

I left the chow hall and went for a walk. As I walked and prayed that day, I realized that all the fights I'd ever been in were about nothing more than pride. I realized that pride was a poor excuse to hurt another person. That day, I made a promise to God that I would never fight again unless it was to protect my family, friends, or my life. Never again would I fight for pride's sake, no matter what.

Several years after this event, in 1975, I was attending a two-year college. A twenty-one-year-old guy who was a bit bigger than me wanted to fight. We were with a couple of young ladies; I think he wanted to impress them. He told me he was sure I hadn't really been in the Marine Corps because I'd just finished serving a mission that summer and was only twenty-one years old myself, and to his reckoning, I was too young to have served in the Marine Corps and served a mission as I said. And I didn't seem very tough to him.

I refused to fight, and he accused me of being afraid.

I said, "Yes, you're right. I am afraid."

Then I left the group as the guy mocked me. I'm sure none of them understood why I was afraid to fight, but I knew God did.

I had six months left of my enlistment and could hardly wait for my discharge and begin to serve a mission by the time I had the fight and seriously hurt the marine who was on KP duty with me. I purchased any and every book I could to facilitate my preparation. One of the books was *So You're Going on a Mission!* (1968) by Barbara Tietjen Jacobs, the title of this chapter. Included in my purchases was the nicest set of leather covered scriptures available. Sometimes, I would open them up and work at reading them. I did okay with a few passages, but most of the scriptures were well beyond my reading abilities.

The conditions under which I was living were anything but conducive to learning and feeling the Spirit of God. The barracks were a base and crude environment at all times of the night and day. I didn't know what to do, but I knew I couldn't prepare to serve others under such conditions. I made numerous attempts to try to find quiet, secluded locations where I could concentrate and feel the Spirit, but it was impossible. Inevitably, someone or something would always disrupt or intrude.

One night, I took my frustration to God and asked for help to be able to focus and read and understand the things I was studying. I must admit I was hoping for a miracle. That's what it would have taken to block out all the distractions in the barracks, lounges, and study areas. To my surprise and disappointment, it didn't happen. I was confused and discouraged, but I kept trying and praying.

A week or so after my prayers for help, as I was walking through the parking lot area, my unit's first sergeant called me over to him. He asked me if as a part of my enlistment I had agreed to be military police for my Military Occupational Specialty (MOS). I told him that I had, but that because of my age, my MOS had been changed to motor vehicle operator. The first sergeant told me that because my MOS had been changed in violation of my enlistment agreement, I was eligible to take part in a special program where I could work and train in a civilian job and live in a private apartment provided by the Marine Corps.

He asked if I was interested, and I replied with an enthusiastic "Yes, of course!" The next thing I knew, I was living in a quiet, private room at the Fallbrook Naval Station and working as a plumber's apprentice. The Fallbrook Naval Station was on the east side of Camp Pendleton, which meant I was close enough to continue attending the single servicemen's branch.

I continued to struggle with the scriptures, which frustrated me. Here within a few months, I was to be teaching the gospel of Jesus Christ, and I could barely read the scriptures.

While attending single adult activities in Carlsbad, I shared my frustration about struggling to read the scriptures with a friend. She told me that her mother had a set of records with several books of scriptures on them and that if I had a record player, she would loan them to me.

It just so happened that one of my major purchases—and a seemingly frivolous one at the time—was a really cool record player with two detachable speakers, a cassette player, and an AM/FM radio. It was one of my most treasured possessions. I accepted my friend's offer and borrowed her mother's record set. I decided that because my reading skills were so poor, I would read every word along with the records.

This proved to be a major turning point in my life. After completing the included books of scriptures, I was able to read with comprehension and understanding. I was able to read other books. I was no speed reader by any means, but it wasn't taking forever to read a single page like it had before.

I took every opportunity to go out and teach people the gospel. The time crept by, but it wasn't long, and finally, I was discharged.

My mother and stepfather had moved to Crestline, Ohio, a year earlier after he was laid off from his job in Utah. Once I was discharged, I flew to Columbus, and my stepfather picked me up and drove to their house.

He had been kind enough to arrange for a job for me on a construction crew in Mansfield. It was a great job. We restored lawns, sprinklers, sidewalks, driveways, and roads that were damaged during gas line leak repairs performed by Columbus Natural Gas.

My supervisor helped the owner of the construction company on his farm, and we worked several hours at the farm on weekends in addition to working full-time construction. I was making good money, which was helpful to fund missionary service.

I had submitted my papers to serve before I was discharged, and they came a few weeks after my arrival in Crestline. To my astonishment, I was to serve in Southern California, the place where I'd just spent the last two years while in the Marine Corps. I knew several of the missionaries who served in the area. It seemed old hat to me. I had imagined serving in an exotic place with unique challenges. I had asked God to send me to the hardest area so I could grow the most.

At that point in time, almost every friend I had was in Southern California, and there were rules that you couldn't correspond with anyone who lived in the area you were serving. This meant I would have to end any communications with all my Southern California friends, including my female friends. By then, all my marine friends had moved on, so I'd lost touch with them.

I even double-checked to make sure there hadn't been a mistake and was assured it was correct. It was a traumatic moment for me, yet with encouragement from my stepfather, I resolved to report and serve.

My mother and stepfather drove me back to Utah to the missionary training center in the first part of July 1973. While he was there, my stepfather applied and was rehired to his former job, so they moved back to Utah just after I entered missionary service.

For the first few months of my mission, I served in the Anaheim area. Then after about six months, the church created two new areas from the previous area. I was transferred to the San Diego area and completed my missionary service there.

Missionary service was challenging for me. I felt like an outcast, and I wasn't accepted or liked by the other missionaries. My service in the Marine Corps had been a cakewalk compared to my serving a mission. I was able to share the gospel with many people and help them choose to be baptized. I was also able to influence several members of the church to return to participation.

Growing up in Kearns, I was very much aware that I was different from the other kids. My church service once again highlighted the differences between me and others serving that had been raised in more traditional homes, and it was painful.

During my missionary service, I only received two letters. Both of them were from my stepfather. Most of the others serving would get one or more letters every few days. At one point, the mission president became aware that I wasn't getting support from home or from friends, so he arranged for my stepfather to call me once a week. It was helpful.

One night at the beginning of my missionary service while still at the training center, those of us preparing to serve were offered blessings by one of the main leaders of the church. I told him about the trouble I had with my ankles and asked for a blessing. He blessed me and said that if I served faithfully, I would never have trouble with my ankles again. I spent twenty out of twenty-four months riding a bicycle up and down the hills of the area during my mission, but I have never had any problems with my ankles. Or did I ever again. Maybe I was a better missionary as I felt I was. I certainly hope so.

CHAPTER 13

What Should I Do?

I returned from serving as a missionary in late June 1975. I was completely lost. Those first few nights in Utah were the roughest of my life. I had no friends, no vehicle, no job, and no prospects for a job considering I was planning to leave for school in two months. I was staying with my mother and stepfather, and as always, it was simply hell to be around my mother. I prayed for help and direction.

My father had moved from Deming to Moses Lake, Washington, while I was in the Marine Corps. Just before I was to leave for missionary service, he called me to offer me a new pickup and a job if I would stop attending church and not serve a mission. I let him know that would never happen and that I had promises to keep.

He and my uncle Tommy now had a water well drilling company in Moses Lake. I called to tell my father that I had completed my service and was now in South Jordan, Utah. Immediately, he offered me a job earning $4 an hour and working as many hours as I wanted. Workdays were at least ten hours a day, often more. He also offered to let me stay on the rig at night as a guard for $25 a night and with meals provided. He said he would fly me to Pasco, Washington, and pick me up at the airport so I could start the next day.

I had eight weeks until school started. In that time, I could earn somewhere around $3,000. That was a lot of money at the time. This was the answer to my prayers. I could get school housing and money to get by until I found a job and started receiving the GI Bill money.

While I served my mission, I was allowed to enroll at a two-year college and was accepted. I was scheduled to start on the first of September. Having only attended a few night classes since the fall of 1970, coupled with my struggles to learn and memorize the scriptures and lessons while serving, I knew I had a lot of groundwork to do, and I felt a two-year college would be a better start for me. I started with remedial English and algebra classes. I decided to become a psychologist. I was going to create "The Waldrop Foundation of Family Relations" and make the world a better place for abused children.

From the very beginning, I enjoyed school. I loved the classes, learning, and activities. For an extrovert and for someone who didn't get to attend high school, this college was a dream come true. There was always something to do, and there were seven girls to every guy. Meeting people and making friends was an everyday thing. I loved to dance, so I took every ballroom dance class I could. Everything was perfect. Then I took my first psychology course, Psychology 101, from Brother Walker. I could not have been more excited.

I walked into the auditorium, selected my seat, and readied myself to take notes. Brother Walker had a presentation projected onto a big screen. The discussion started with several pictures that could be interpreted in several ways or had several views of different depictions in the same drawing. He then pointed out that we perceive or interpret things based on our experiences and programming.

It felt as though he was moving too fast, and I was losing much of what he was saying. I resolved to attend every lecture and read the course books and assigned reading several times until I understood everything completely. I did just that.

Then came the first test. I was concerned, but I had prepared and thought I was ready. As always, I did one of my begging prayers. I took the test and miserably failed. I was horrified. Psychology was my major. How could I do so poorly? I had read every bit of my assignment and listened intently to every word Brother Walker spoke, but I still failed.

But it was only the first quiz, I thought to myself. *I'd do better next time. I'd read more, take better notes, and listen more closely to the lectures.* I did all those things. I also prayed more earnestly. It didn't help. I failed the second quiz, followed by the third. By that time, the deadline to drop the course was upon me. In desperation, I chose to drop that course before it affected my grades, hoping to somehow take it in the future and do better.

At the next opportunity, I registered for Psychology 101 again, and Brother Walker was again the instructor. This time, I walked into the auditorium feeling great trepidation and praying with all intent. This was a make-or-break for my dream of becoming a psychologist.

I took a seat. I readied myself to take notes and listen carefully. Brother Walker started his lecture. He presented the exact same information. This time, to my great surprise, it all made sense. I read the assignments, and they all made sense too. I didn't feel rushed, lost, or that the information was coming too fast. I took each of the tests I'd previously failed, but this time I did well. With that, I had stumbled upon one of the greatest lessons of my life. Because of my poor education foundation and the way my mind worked, many things easily confounded and confused me. From the time I dropped that first psychology course to attending the course a second time, I hadn't picked up a psychology book or listened to a word of psychology lectures. So why did it make sense this time and why could I manage the information?

I realized that the first time around, I'd never heard or considered the concepts. I had no reference points or system to manage the information. During the time between the first course and taking it a second time, my subconscious had organized the information and created a place to file it for recall as needed. I would use this lesson many times when I had a course that I had little to no knowledge or experience in. Sometimes, I attended or audited courses I felt I might struggle with and then dropped them before they could negatively affect my grades.

When the summer break came, I desperately didn't want to go back to stay with my mother and stepfather, but I had little choice. I determined to work two jobs so I wouldn't be home much. My first job was as an assistant manager at Household Finance, a small loan company. I did well, especially on debt collections. After a few weeks, I got a second job as a security guard for Burns Security.

On my first night working security, I was assigned to guard an equipment yard for EMCO mining equipment. I was to be there for four hours. At the time, the workers of the company were on strike. I'd only been on the job for one hour when a car pulled up and four men got out. They proceeded to pull rifles out of the car's trunk and began shooting at the equipment.

Bullets ricocheted and zipped across the yard. I drove to the ground and crawled behind a small building, yelling the whole time that there were people in the yard. The men got into the car and sped away. As soon as I was sure it was safe, I got my boss on the phone and quit.

The next week, my father called and asked if I would work for him in Nebraska for more money than I could have made in the same amount of time doing both the security and Household Finance jobs. I accepted and drove to Nebraska. I worked for about two weeks and made good money.

Things were different between us now. My father hadn't laid a hand on me in over six years, and I was now a US marine. Once when I was working for him in Nebraska, he became angry at me and drew back his fist to hit me. I was putting nuts on the studs of the drill stem piping. I did not flinch or react. I turned my head just enough so that he knew I could see his fist.

I simply shook my head and calmly said "You don't want to do that" and kept working.

He dropped his fist and stood there looking at me, silent. It felt good to stand up to him without fear, rudeness, threats, or harshness. He knew it too.

It turned out that the place in Nebraska where we were drilling after about seventy feet in depth became cemented rock. The reverse rotary drilling rig we used wasn't capable of drilling through cemented rock. It was great for drilling through sand, gravel, and dirt but not solid or cemented rock. We were dead in the water. The job only lasted about a week and a half, and soon I was on my way back to Utah with a few weeks left before school started and no job prospects.

I should have stayed the summer in Idaho. That was the summer of 1976 when the Teton Dam broke and flooded the whole valley. There was plenty of work, and I missed it all.

My second year at college went by in a flash. I decided to transfer to a university and started as soon as I graduated with an associate of science degree in psychology. By the end of my second year at college, I was twenty-three and tired of being alone. It had been seven years since I'd left Deming to return to Kearns. I hadn't felt a part of a family since I was eleven, and I wanted to find someone, get married, and have children.

I met a nice girl. She was forgetful and naive, but she was pretty. She was also petite and seemed congenial; she went along with everything. It seemed as though we would get along well. Frankly, I was plain stupid. I remember thinking that she was safe because she was so petite—that even if she beat me, it wouldn't hurt. We married at the end of August 1977.

After the wedding, she told me she really loved her high school boyfriend and only married me because she knew I would provide better than he would. I thought that when she saw how hard I worked and how much I loved and cared for her, she would change her mind and love me. In fact, her lack of love and commitment created greater hurt and pain than I had ever known.

My schoolwork began to suffer because I was rescuing her from one idiotic incident after another. I remember thinking she should really love me because I was so helpful and made her life better. I thought of myself as her white knight.

Soon after that, several things happened that highlighted her lack of commitment to the relationship, her irresponsibility, and her inability to handle problems or issues. These things had worried me before we married, and a few weeks before marrying, I had feelings it was the wrong thing to do, but I decided it was just cold feet. On the morning we were married, I got a sick feeling like I'd just made the biggest mistake of my life.

Things quickly went from crazy to completely insane. Everything turned into chaos. By December, I had decided to quit psychology because I had too many problems of my own to help anyone else. Quitting school soon followed, and I needed work to support the family. By December, she was pregnant. I was excited to be fathering a baby, and I was intent on providing well and taking care of my little family.

By the middle of January 1978, I had arranged to move to Moses Lake and work for my father. Things went well for about three months. In April, the drilling jobs slowed down, but my father kept coming each morning to pick me up for work. I worked at his shop repairing, cleaning, and organizing the rig or at his farm repairing equipment, fences, and such.

Payday came and went, and I didn't receive a check. When I asked my father about getting paid, what he said floored me. He said I wouldn't be getting any pay for the last month because we hadn't really been working at drilling wells. He added that I wouldn't be getting a paycheck for several weeks after we started drilling again. I quit on the spot.

I didn't know how I was going to make ends meet or feed my family. Down the hill from where we lived, one of our neighbors had a garden. He had passed away several weeks before my work situation developed, so rather than just letting the vegetables go to waste, I harvested what I could. I walked the ditches and canals for asparagus, poached rabbits, and went fishing. Each time I went out to get food, I prayed. As soon as I had what we needed, I thanked God for the blessing. We didn't go hungry.

The day after my father informed me I wasn't getting paid, I went looking for work and found a good-paying job mixing cattle feed. Sugar beets were a major crop in the area, and this company bought sugar beet molasses and mixed vitamins, medications, and such. The mix was then pumped into lick pots or sprayed on feed at the fields or lots where the cattle were located. The job mostly entailed picking up fifty- to one-hundred-pound sacks off pallets and lifting them onto a big mixing tank with a grate that had a blade that cut the sacks. Then I'd lift the ends, emptying the contents into the mixer. Part of my job also included cleaning piping and storage tanks of sediment with shovels and loading and cleaning trucks.

One morning, I woke up in more pain than I'd ever felt before. It was my lower back. I couldn't bend over. I could barely stand. As I attempted to dress, I tried to reach my blue jeans but couldn't bend over enough to reach them. I called my wife and asked her to help me.

"You aren't much of a man if you can't put your own pants on," she said.

Her words hurt deeper than anything anyone had ever said to me. Unable to count on her help, I went to the closet and got two wire hangers. I pulled them straight, with the hooks at the bottom, then hooked the belt loops on each side of my jeans and shimmied them up around my waist. Then I pulled my belt as tight as I could and went to work.

I was in tremendous pain that day, but it didn't stop me from doing my work. At one point, I was asked to help two other employees move a full fifty-five-gallon drum. One of the workers pulled it too much in his direction, and it was about to fall on top of him. Instinctually, I grabbed it and pulled it back upright. When I did, it twisted my back, and it popped all the way from the bottom to the top. It almost sounded like a machine gun going off. At first, I was worried that I had done more harm, but it relieved much of the pain.

I went to a chiropractor who adjusted me and gave me relief from the pain for a short time. Over the next twenty-six years, anytime I felt pain or pressure in my back, I would adjust myself using chairs or stairs handrails as needed to apply the correct pressure to align my back. When that no longer worked, I went to an orthopedic surgeon who took an MRI and determined I had 6 mm for my spinal cord, but I was supposed to have 15 mm. Surgery revealed that I had ruptured two disks, but that in the intervening twenty-six years, the vertebrae had become fused with bone. All they could do was eliminate the back pressure by cutting bone away.

My oldest son, Paul the II, was born at the end of August 1978 while we were living in Moses Lake. I worked at the cattle feed job for several months before my father approached me again, offering me a guaranteed monthly salary regardless of what he had me do.

The money would be better than what I was making at the cattle feed, so I agreed.

I went back to work for my father. This time, we stayed busy. Working with him was always a challenge because of his lack of patience and flash anger. In November 1978, just a week before Thanksgiving, I was working on finishing an adobe room that would attach to a large doublewide manufactured home he'd bought and was moving to his farm on Dotson Road, west of Moses Lake. I'd been working alone for several hours while he went to town for materials. When he got back, I made a suggestion about how we might do something different to save time and be more functional, to which he reacted by raising his fist and then putting it down quickly.

"You're not paid to think," he snapped. "Just shut up and do what you're told!"

I'd had enough. "Fine," I replied. Then I told him I would never work for him again under any circumstance, and I walked out.

Since he'd been my ride to work, I would have to do the twenty-five miles back home on foot. I had a cold that morning, and on top of that, I'd neglected to wear a coat sufficient for the weather. By the time I made it to I-90, it had begun to snow, and with the wind, I found myself chilled. I found several onions on the side of the road and ate them to relieve my stuffy nose and sore throat. It helped.

I put out my thumb and caught a ride into Moses Lake then home. I told my wife that we were moving back to Utah. That I would no longer work for my father no matter what. We packed our belongings into a U-Haul trailer, and in two days, we were on our way.

Once we got to Utah, I found work with a drilling company. The new job required me to travel out of town several weeks out of the month. The problem was little Paul wasn't getting the care a small baby needed. I decided to look for work that would allow me to be home for little Paul. I found a machinist helper's job in a water purification equipment manufacturing company. The money wasn't as good, but I was home every evening to care for him. We moved to a house on Seventh East and just north of the I-80 on-ramp.

After working at the manufacturing job for a few months, my wife met some friends who were working as foster parents to juvenile criminals. These teenage boys had committed petty crimes and could no longer stay in their homes. My wife thought we could supplement our income by becoming foster parents ourselves, but I wasn't keen on the idea. Still, I listened to the proposals. As it turned out, the foster parent service company was in negotiations to establish a youth ranch with my wife's friends and another couple who had ranching experience, thus their interest in me.

I decided the proposal sounded too good to turn down. We would be given a house to live in on the east side of Bear Lake, Utah, where we would house and be compensated for two boys, in addition to being allowed to continue working a regular job.

With our minds made up, we loaded up our household goods and moved just north of Laketown, Utah. It was a beautiful area, and I enjoyed living there. As always, things were not as promised. The first few boys that were placed with us weren't bad kids, but the next few were horrible. There was an arsonist, a child molester, and a murderer. Worst of all, we had been misled as to the nature of their offenses when they were placed in our home.

Little Paul turned one year old on the ranch. Because of the neglectful nature of my wife and the issues with the boys, things had gotten bad. Several times, the managers of the youth program counseled me to take little Paul and leave, that my wife really didn't care and wouldn't come after us.

I didn't leave with little Paul, mostly because I was afraid my wife's well-to-do parents would insist, she get custody, and I wasn't willing to risk losing him. There were other reasons, the chief of which was my own history with my family. I was the only child from my parents' first marriage, and I was often introduced as "this is only my half-brother." This hurt deeply, and I didn't want that to happen to little Paul.

It was not long before I decided to quit and move to a house we rented in Laketown, Utah. It was a pleasant little house, but it had no insulation, and we couldn't keep it heated. I had gotten a job at Stauffer Chemicals Phosphorus Milling plant east of Laketown and north of Randolph, Utah. It was a good job. I operated front-end loaders, plant process equipment, and drove the delivery truck as a relief driver.

It had been two years since I'd quit school and psychology. I didn't feel I wanted to go back into psychology, but I wanted to get my bachelor's degree in something. I wasn't sure what I wanted to do. All I knew was that I wanted to do something. I thought a lot about it. I still had enough left from the GI Bill to finish.

In the spring of 1980, a trailer came up for rent in Round Valley, just west of Laketown. It was small, just eight feet wide and forty feet long, and was on the south end of the valley in the mouth of Cottonwood Canyon. It was a beautiful location; the water source was a natural spring, and the rent was only seventy-five dollars per month—half of what the house in Laketown rented for. And we'd even be able to keep it warm. We moved in just as soon as we could.

The closest neighbor was at least a half-mile away. I would take little Paul on my back for hikes, and where the trail was safe, I let him walk on his own. I installed a small woodstove in the trailer, cut wood for the stove, and we stayed warm all winter long. For meals, I hunted grouse, ducks, rabbits, and deer. Not long after that, several friends from Laketown approached me, telling me I couldn't live in Round Valley.

"Why not?" I asked.

They told me that there was a family named Price in Round Valley that would catch people by themselves and beat them up. They burned barns down or egg houses and buildings.

I listened to my friends and finally said, "You all don't understand. It's not me that needs to be afraid. It's them." They just shook their heads.

Three months later, my wife was pregnant with our second child when we decided to take a trip to Logan, Utah, to get groceries and other things we needed. It was after midnight on a Saturday when we arrived back home. We unloaded our car and went inside. My wife and little Paul were lying on the couch resting before going to bed, and I was sitting beside them. All of a sudden, we heard the sound of loud whooping, hollering, pounding on the trailer, and glass breaking.

The first thing I saw was the fear in the eyes of my wife and son. I was enraged.

"Where's my gun?" I yelled. "I'm going to kill someone!"

I grabbed my 270, loaded my last two rounds, and opened the door. Two people were running away from my little trailer and toward the road. I drew a bead on one then had the thought that if I shot one, I'd go to jail, so I shot over his head instead. Then I shot toward their pickup. They jumped into their pickup, started it up, and took off.

I set the gun down and grabbed the keys to my car, ran outside, jumped in the car, and followed after them. I followed their taillights as they headed east toward Laketown and out of sight. I knew who they were from their pickup. It was the Price family I'd been warned about. I decided to turn around and go back home and have a talk with them the next day.

The next morning, we went to church as usual. When we got home, I took off my suit coat and tie and unbuttoned my shirt collar and sleeves. I then rolled up my sleeves and told my wife to go ahead and fix lunch. I would be right back, I told her. I was going to talk to the Price family. I was going to explain that they needed to leave us alone, that I was not like other people and would never tolerate my family being attacked or harmed.

I was six-two and weighed 240 pounds. My measurements were twenty-six-inch calves, twenty-nine-inch thighs, thirty-four-inch waist, fifty-inch chest, twenty-two-inch biceps, and nineteen-inch neck. I had worked on large drilling rigs lifting three-hundred-pound slips by myself with either hand and operated a 150-pound set of tongs. I was all muscle.

When I got to their house, there were several of them outside working on a car parked on the public road. I drove past them and parked on the road. I got out and asked to talk to their father.

As he walked toward me, I told him that a couple of his sons had come to my place at about midnight last night whooping, hollering, pounding on the trailer, and breaking glass. He said that it hadn't been his sons. I told him that I saw them and knew it was them, but he only argued. Then I told him that they needed to understand I wasn't like their other neighbors and would not tolerate harassment and attacks of any kind.

He rushed me, pushing with his hands on my chest, but I faded back then forward to my previous position. I told him not to push me, to which he ran forward again and shoved me. I told him that pushing me a third time wouldn't be pleasant and that I would protect myself and my family with a fury he'd never experienced.

He didn't listen and came at me and pushed me a third time. This time, after fading backward, I came forward with a crushing blow with my right fist to his neck and shoulder, sending him down. By that time a third came at me and, I sent him to the ground with a right blow, a fourth one came running out of the house, followed by a fifth, who was a family friend.

I sent the fourth one down and was about to do the same to the fifth when I tripped over one of the ones on the ground and went down. I looked up just in time to see a fist with a big longhorn cattle ring coming at me. It broke my nose.

I ducked my head and covered it with my arms while all five pounded on my back, head, and arms. Blindly, I reached up and grabbed the first head of hair I could feel, taking a good solid hold and snapping the head to the ground. Out of the corner of my eye, I watched a set of feet fly into midair.

As soon as he was on the ground, I twisted his neck and yelled to the others, "If you don't get off of me, I'll kill him!"

The guy I had started yelling, "Get off! Get off! He's gonna kill me!" He was the youngest of the five but weighed at least two hundred pounds.

They backed off, and I got to my feet, still holding my captive by the hair. I pulled him up and punched him with my free hand then shoved him at the others. Once I was on my feet, I took to holding the discussion on my terms. Suddenly, they all left the fight. The next thing I knew, all five were standing thirty to forty feet away from me. They had each gone and gotten a weapon like a tire iron, crescent wrench, or wood club. When I took a step, they took a step back.

If they were not coming at me, I would not go at them, and I told them as much. I then started to explain how I wasn't like other people. I must admit I used my Marine Corps words and not my church words.

I told them, "I've heard about you. This time, you've messed with a person who knows how to mess. If you burn me out, there'll be a bigger fire at your place. If you so much as hurt one of mine, I'll kill every one of you."

Then I told them that if they hurt me, there was a bunch of Damn Hillbilly Waldrops who can't even read who would come into this valley and kill anyone with their last name, whether they were related or not. That part may have been a stretch, but I wanted to instill as much fear in them as possible. I told them that I had friends in this valley and they'd better not mess with them either. Then I told them, "If I walk in, you better walk out!"

With that, I turned and walked away. Just as I got to my car, an ambulance drove up. Apparently, when the neighbors saw me go to the house, and because of the Price family's reputation, they called me an ambulance. Later, I heard they had to call another because they couldn't get all five of them into one, but I am not sure of that.

Things were quiet for a while after that. I continued to work on the drilling rigs, barely scraping by. I had cut a whole winter supply of wood and hunted for game to feed the family. Having gone to college for three years and not having a degree or career weighed heavily on my mind. As I worked, drove, and hiked, the question of "What should I do?" was constantly on my mind.

I prayed and sought direction from God. One day, while I was cutting wood, the thought came to me that I should become a welding engineer. I had no idea what a welding engineer did, but I kept thinking about it. Later, while driving toward Brigham City with little Paul in the car, I began to think about how the car was welded together and that welding engineers must design how welds were made.

Having done welding, I knew there were different types of coating on electrodes and different types of welding rods. Someone had to figure out how and when to apply the different welding electrodes and types. I decided to become a welding engineer. Now I just had to figure out how to get back to school and where I needed to go.

I started to think of the things I needed to go back to school. I had two sons now, one twenty-six months old and one two months old. I decided I needed a vinyl-covered hide-a-bed couch. I kept my eyes out for one and finally saw an advertisement in the nickel ads. I called the number and introduced myself. There was a long uncomfortable silence.

"Are you still there?" I asked.

The voice at the other end replied, "Yeah, sir, do you know who this is?"

"No," replied.

"This is Gary," the man informed me. He was the father of the Price family. "Is it okay if we talk?"

"Sure," I said. "As long as we're courteous and respectful, I don't hold grudges."

We decided to meet outside of the property I was renting. The first thing he said to me was, "I want to apologize. I talked to my boys, and they admitted to coming to your place to try to scare you off so they could rent the trailer. We never want to fight with you again. That was like trying to fight an oak tree!"

We made our peace, and I ended up buying his couch.

I continued to work the drilling rigs as a floor hand, and it was now November of 1980. It was commonplace for a relief crew to not show up and for us to work twenty-four hours straight. That wasn't as bad as the fact the crew I worked with consisted of a drugged-out driller named John who pulled dangerously life-threatening stunts one after another. The other floor hand was a thirty-nine-year-old guy named Dave who was probably the laziest rig worker I ever knew. The floor hand helper was named Jimmy. He was fifty-five and a nice guy, but he couldn't do much work. I was fairly sure both Jimmy and Dave were alcoholics.

There were countless shifts where the relief crews didn't show up for two days. I was so exhausted from doing 90 percent of the work that at the end of the forty-eight hours, I could barely drag myself to my car to go home.

One night after a forty-eight-hour shift, I found a message waiting for me at home. The tool pusher wanted to talk to me. I called him back, and he told me something had come up and the relief crew had to be relieved. I would have to be back in four hours. I fibbed and told him I was already halfway to my in-laws and couldn't get back until the next morning. I put the kids in the car, got my wife in the car, and we drove directly to the in-laws' house where I slept for twelve hours straight.

The next morning, I got up early, took my family back to Round Valley, and drove to the drill site. I went into the doghouse to change into my work clothes. As I entered through the door, Dave the lazy guy started in on me for not being there the day before.

"Was it hard to actually have to work without me to carry your load?" I snapped at him, to which he responded by pushing me into the lockers.

As I shoved him away, I said, "Never touch me again, or I'll wad you into a little ball and toss you in the sagebrush."

I went to my locker and changed into my work clothes. As I went to leave the doghouse, he was still in front of his locker, and he butted me with his behind. That was it! I swung around and picked him up in the middle of his chest by the overalls. I carried him like a suitcase outside and across the snow-covered parking lot to the burn pit, which was full of burned bentonite sacks. I swung him twice and let go. He flew through the air, screaming, and landed in the burned bentonite sacks. I remember thinking it was pretty the way the black ashes swirled up around him. I figured I'd be fired, so I went to my car and drove home.

Three days later, I went back to the drill rig to get my last check. The tool pusher wanted to talk to me, so I went into his trailer.

"You know I've got to fire you, don't you?" he asked.

"I figured as much," I said.

"I can't have someone who throws people in the burn pit," he added.

"I know," I said. "But as long as I'm leaving, you should know I've been doing this kind of work since I was fourteen, and I've never worked with a more careless and stupid driller. I think he's on drugs. The old man is sweet but can't do an hour's worth of work. The other guy is the laziest individual I've ever worked with. He pretty much forced me to do all the work just to get it done. He also physically attacked me twice before I threw him into the burn pit. If it weren't for the driller, he couldn't hold the job."

The tool pusher nodded and said, "Well, I still have to let you go."

He handed me my check and I left. Now I was in a fix. I had a wife, two boys, a dog, a cat, and a parakeet. How was I going to provide?

CHAPTER 14

Turn Around and Go Register

I left the drill site and began the fifty-mile drive back to our little trailer. My last check would last us for a few weeks, but I could
expect no unemployment compensation. On the drive, I felt the full
weight of the world on me. I had a family to provide for. I needed to
somehow get back to school so I could create a future and security
for myself and my family.

I was determined to rewrite the legacy my parents had written
for me. But at that moment, all the evil mistreatment, beatings, and
criticisms I'd received in my life felt justified. I hadn't finished college. I was barely getting by. I'd just been fired. I had no idea how to
go forward and accomplish any of my goals. I prayed, begged, and
prayed again all the way back home.

I started looking for work the very next day. It was close to
Thanksgiving, and we were living in rural Rich County where there
wasn't an abundance of jobs. Almost all work required travel of forty
to ninety miles. In keeping with my nature, I kept searching.

Then on Christmas Eve, a drill crew showed up at the door of
our trailer. The tool pusher who'd fired me sent them. They told me
that my entire old crew had been fired and that he wanted me to
come back to work.

This was a wonderful Christmas present. I was employed again,
and I had been vindicated. I agreed to start Christmas night.

We enjoyed our Christmas Eve and Christmas Day. Then in the afternoon, I got my meals and gear ready and waited for the crew to pick me up for work. When the car pulled up, I went outside, the driver's side back door swung open, and I went to climb inside. But before I could, I heard a whisper.

"Don't get in the vehicle."

I stood up straight and thought to myself that this was silly. I really needed the job. So I started to climb in, and once again, the whisper came.

"Don't get in the vehicle."

I told the crew I couldn't get in and wouldn't be working on the rig.

I was back in the same fix and running out of money and had no job. I kept looking for work, but nothing was coming, and I felt a growing pressure to somehow get back to school and become a welding engineer.

New Year's 1981 came and went. The next Monday, we decided to go to Logan, Utah, for groceries. We had WIC vouchers and twenty-five dollars in the checking account. A friend needed to go to town as well, so we took her.

We started at about eight in the morning and exited Logan Canyon on Highway 89 a little over an hour later. As we passed Utah State University, there was a large sign on the north side of the road that read "Registration Today, Jan. 5, 1981."

As I glanced back to the road, I heard a whisper say, "Turn around and go register."

I retorted in my mind, "I have no money. I can't go register."

The whisper came again. "Turn around and go register."

"I have no money," I reiterated, but the whisper said again, "Turn around and go register."

When we came to a stoplight, I pulled into the left turn lane and made a U-turn.

The questions came from both my wife and her friend, "Why are we turning around?"

I told them that I had to go register for school.

"How are you going to do that?" they both asked.

"I don't know!" I answered.

I drove onto the campus and found the administration building. I parked and went in. I was directed downstairs where I said that I needed to register to attend college. I told them I had graduated from college in the spring of 1977, had attended a summer and fall semester in 1977 at a university, and that I hadn't attended college since then.

I was told I could register un-matriculated for fifteen dollars until my transcripts arrived. With that, I went back out to the car, got a check from the checkbook, and recorded a fifteen-dollar check to Utah State University in our register. I then told my wife to go pick up the WIC food for the kids and not to spend any more than eight dollars. That left two dollars in our account. I told them to come back as soon as they were done and wait for me. I was starting school, and we would need to move to Logan. My wife and her friend left to pick up the needed groceries.

I went back inside and gave them a check for fifteen dollars. Next, I went to the financial aid department to get my GI Bill support started. After a quick discussion, I was told I needed to register for classes before I could apply for the GI Bill. I was directed to a building where I explained to the people assisting students with registering that I need to become a welding engineer. I was given suggested courses, and I registered for eighteen credits and returned to the finical aid office, and I completed the GI bill paperwork.

The financial aid counselor then told me it would take two or three months for the money to start coming. My heart fell. Fear and confusion flashed into my mind. Then the thought came to me: I had done everything I was directed, and I knew something would work out.

I thanked the finical aid counselor, gathered my things, and got up to leave. As I reached for the door, the counselor asked me, "By the way, would a five-hundred-dollar loan each month help until your GI Bill money arrives? Then you can easily repay the loan."

While almost overcome by tears, relief rushed through my being. I returned to his desk, and we completed the loan documents. I was given a five-hundred-dollar check and sent on my way. I told my wife all about the loan that would make my return to college possible. We both agreed we needed to get an apartment right away. We picked up several newspapers and called every apartment listed. All were taken. Then we called on a studio apartment that was still available, and we rented it on the spot.

When we got back to Laketown, we called the church leaders, and the members helped us. Church members provided us with a truck and horse trailer in which all our goods and furniture were loaded, and the next day, we moved to Logan. Fortunately, there was enough storage in part of the basement next to our little studio apartment that we could store the items that wouldn't fit in the apartment.

I was two days late when I showed up for classes. Dr. Long of the Technology Department was assigned as my guidance counselor, and he was quite put off that I would have the audacity to show up for classes two days late. He told me that he expected anybody who would show up two days late to fail. My attempts to explain and to assure him that was not the case fell on deaf ears. In fact, I think he did all he could to make his predictions come true.

After my meeting with Dr. Long, I went into the common area of the technology building where several of my classmates were discussing the courses we were taking.

Someone next to me said, "I think it's great that we're in one of the top-three rated welding engineering schools in the nation."

I must have sounded like an absolute idiot when I suddenly exclaimed, "You mean to tell me this is a welding engineering school?"

Everybody looked at me with expressions of dismay and disdain. I was astounded and thrilled. Without any knowledge or planning, I'd been led to the very place and school where I needed to be. I may have seemed like a fool to the others there, but I didn't care. I knew the complete story! I knew what God had done for me, and how things appeared was of little consequence.

I stayed in the program until I graduated in June of 1982. The coursework at the beginning was challenging. Switching from social science to physical science was demanding, and I had to take courses when they were offered, or I'd have to postpone my graduation. With a family including two sons under four years old, postponing was not an option.

After my first two quarters at Utah State, I still had 101 credits to complete in order to graduate. I felt driven to graduate after the spring quarter, so I worked out a schedule with Dr. Long who remained skeptical.

I took eighteen credits in the summer quarter, twenty credits in the fall, twenty-one in the winter, and twenty-four in the spring. Things went as planned. I even made the dean's list, receiving a B+ in one class and coming just short of a 4.0 GPA.

That last year, I had so many books I couldn't carry them all, so I mapped out my daily route and created book/study stops. I would stage the books I would need for the next couple of courses at my book/study stops. As the schedule allowed, I would stop and study as I needed to participate in the courses. I had no time to waste.

All that year, I had a recurring nightmare. In my nightmare, I would be dutifully attending classes, studying, and doing okay. Suddenly, I realized I'd forgotten to attend a class, had missed too many tests, or would be failing the class and, therefore, couldn't graduate. I would wake up in a sweat and double-check my schedule and grades before I could relax and go back to sleep—something that for me was a rarity during that time.

I was getting close to graduation, so I visited the professor that was supervising a correspondence course I was required to take, a four-credit management psychology course. I had completed five or six of the assignments and had come up with a plan to complete the remaining eleven assignments and three required essays in the next several weeks.

It was a Thursday afternoon. I shared the plan with my professor who looked at me and said, "Paul, you don't understand. You must hand in and pass all eleven remaining assignments and three essays by Monday or you can't graduate in June."

I was overwhelmed. Not only would I have to complete that coursework in four days, but I also had classes to attend on Friday from 8:00 a.m. to 5:00 p.m.—and those classes had assignments due as well. I also had to study a two-inch-thick course book. Still, I was determined that I was not going to fail and that I would graduate on time in June.

I decided to stay awake for the next four days and nights, using every moment to get all the required coursework done. I knew it was going to be torturous and would take everything I had.

I asked a friend for a blessing that Thursday evening. After the blessing, I started on the unfinished coursework. On Friday morning, I went to my classes as scheduled. That night, I got home, ate, and went to work.

I stole an hour or two of sleep here and there. Saturday morning was as daunting a day as any in my life. I worked straight through four on Sunday morning. Since I was asking for God's blessings in my efforts, I felt I needed to go to my Sunday meetings as part of my commitment.

After I got back home, I went straight back to my coursework. By midnight, I'd completed all eleven assignments and three essays. There was still more coursework to do in my other classes, so I buckled down and was finished by 4 a.m. This gave me time for just three hours of sleep before going to class.

It felt rather good to walk into the professor's office and hand in all the remaining eleven assignments and three essays. He asked me how I did it.

"I just stayed up and did it," I replied.

I turned in all the other coursework assignments due and did well on those assignments. The lowest grade I received was a B. I had done it. I was going to graduate.

CHAPTER 15

Be Patient, I Am Blessing You

Everything was going well, and graduation was scheduled for June 1982. There were about eight of us in my class due to graduate. Each of us was submitting résumés to any listed job opening. There was an opening working at the Wolf Creek Nuclear Power Plant, which was under construction. The job was for a beginning construction engineer for Daniels Construction.

I had submitted a résumé but hadn't heard back yet. Then sometime in the middle of May, I got a call from a recruiter for Daniels International offering me a job without even interviewing me. It was a good job with reasonable pay, and I jumped on the opportunity. It was in Burlington, Kansas.

As it turned out, only me and one other graduate had jobs upon graduation. The others all found jobs soon after, which was a relief. Since leaving home, I had relocated numerous times between the Marine Corps, church service, school, and work. The last big move had been from was from Round Valley to Logan for school. We then moved next door to a two-bedroom apartment, which was perfect for my little family. Even that move took considerable effort.

I was overjoyed to learn that the new job included relocation, including moving and travel expenses. All we did was watch as movers and a moving van arrived, packed our goods, and loaded them up for shipment.

Graduation was one of my proudest moments. I was determined to rewrite my part of the Waldrop legacy. My father didn't place value on education and had little but criticism for my efforts. Still I proudly walked and received my diploma. I even had a portrait taken of me in my graduation gown, cap, and orange tassel. I wanted my kids and grandkids to have a visual reminder of that accomplishment.

We decided to live in Emporia, Kansas. It took a couple of days to drive there from Logan. We found an apartment and moved in. The job was exciting. My first assignment was as a completion engineer, in which I followed up on uncompleted construction projects and resolved any issues with them. I also created dispositions for engineering change notices and nonconformance reports.

After a few months, one of the senior engineers commented that I "must be pretty proud." The question startled me. I had no idea what he was talking about. I was unaware of the fact that the supervisor kept statistics on the approval and rejection rates of the writing and dispositioning of the engineering change notices (design changes) and nonconformance reports. I had a 100 percent acceptance or approval rate for both. Because of that, the other individuals in the group were irritated.

As it turned out, my practical side caused me to have an unusual ability to resolve problems. That ability took my career to places I could have never imagined. Soon after the senior engineer's comments, I was transferred to the quality engineering group. This group was tasked with resolving various quality and inspection issues. I really enjoyed the group. I had a lot to learn, and this provided the experience I needed to learn.

Not long after joining the quality engineering group, I was tasked with writing several nuclear documentation and process procedures. I had no idea how to go about writing such procedures, but I was given a stack of codes and standards from which I was to glean the requirements and actions required to perform the work. I think I was given the assignment because none of the other engineers had the determination and patience. I accomplished the assignment with only a few grammatical and spelling errors.

One of the tasks of quality engineering was supporting the quality inspectors and addressing any issues that arose. An issue where the inspectors were not able to measure acutely skewed tee fillet welds on piping supports was identified, and I was assigned to resolve the problem. I met with several of the inspectors, and we looked at designs and several examples in the field. There were several gauges that measured both ninety degrees and obtuse fillet weld. I researched industry gauges to determine if there were any available that could measure acute angles, but there were none.

I then decided to create something that would accurately measure acute skewed tee fillet welds and came up with the Fillet Keys. The Fillet Keys were simple. They were made of flat stainless steel and were 1/8 inch thick, 3 inches long, and had a small hole on the end for a key ring. They were machined to the standard height of the specified in fillet weld designs height. The various sizes of the Fillet Keys were connected by a keychain. They worked wonderfully, and we created a dozen sets. The inspectors were pleased.

Because I worked for Daniels Construction when I invented the Fillet Keys, they owned the idea and all rights to the gauges. The company wasn't interested in patenting or manufacturing the gauges, so I approached them and asked how much it would cost me to buy the rights. I was told that I could buy all rights for ten dollars, and they drew up a contract. I wrote them a check and became the proud owner of my first invention. I had no idea how to go about patenting, manufacturing, or marketing, but I was excited.

A few months later, I was offered a job as a plant engineer with Kansas Gas and Electric, the managing owner of the Wolf Creek Nuclear Power Plant. This was a great opportunity and gave me the chance to learn how an operating plant was managed.

The work was long and demanding, and it was shift work, which meant I had to endure long nights. When it was slow, I thought about the skew tee fillet weld issue. There was also an issue with measuring obtuse angles as well and assuring the fillets were of the specified sizes. One problem was that depending on the included angle, the size of the skewed tee fillet weld needed to be increased. We would need to measure from 0° to 180° angles.

One night as I was walking and thinking about the issue, an idea occurred to me. What if there was a way to measure the included angle and the fillet leg size at the same time and any need to increase leg size was predetermined? That would be valuable. The only problem was that a gauge that could do both would be too large and cumbersome.

I researched all the commercially available protractors and found nothing that would work. I thought about the size of dial face it would take to make my idea work and determined it would need to be about a half inch in diameter. It would also need to be able to measure accurately within two and one-half degrees. That would make it unlikely to be able to read because of the increments being too close to each other and would appear as a solid line.

As I continued to ponder the problem, the idea came to me that if I made a mark on a round dial face that was pointing to one side on a scale and I drew a line directly through the middle of the dial face to the opposite side of the scale, it would divide the scale in half. That allowed one side of the scale to start at 0° and progress to 180° by five-degree increments and the other side of the scale to start at 2.5° and progress to 180° by five-degree increments. I had invented the Easy Set Protractor. The protractor made the idea of using slide rules work, and within the week, I invented the Universal Weld Gauge. It measured every aspect of all types of welds. As its name indicated, it was universal.

By this time, my financial situation had improved greatly. I took the money and hired an attorney to secure a patient. The attorney seemed to take forever, so I contacted him several times. I finally discovered that he'd done something to get himself disbarred, which resulted in me losing all the money. He promised to pay me back as soon as he could, but I never saw a penny.

One of the great epiphanies of my life occurred to me during my time in Kansas. It was a shock; I was not prepared. It happened when I was installing a new clutch in our 1979 Subaru. I'll always remember the moment that I reached to move the engine forward when the epiphany struck like a ton of bricks.

It was I'd done everything I could do to earn the love and respect of my parents, and I would never get it. I had served two years in the Marine Corps without any disciplinary actions. With one more year, I would have been awarded a good-conduct medal. I had honorably served God. I graduated from college with an associate's in science degree as well as from Utah State University with a bachelor's degree in science in metallurgical-welding technology. I had worked at the Wolf Creek Nuclear Power Plant for three years. I had created three inventions that looked promising to result create wealth. None of these accomplishments earned any consideration from my mother or father.

I then realized I could never do anything that would make a difference to them. It was clear that their feelings and treatment of me had nothing to do with me. I represented the two things they hated the most: "themselves and each other." I was the unavoidable reminder of the destroyed hopes and dreams of their youth. Their hatred and anger for each other was the root of all the mistreatment, name-calling, beatings, and abuse I experienced.

I had been self-driven my entire life to somehow earn their love and respect and realizing that was impossible left me completely lost. For a time, I lacked a reason and motivation to move forward. I finally concluded that I was who I was, and I would just see how much I could achieve for the sake of self-improvement and accomplishment.

I was burned out working at Wolf Creek. For over two years, I had been making the two-hour drive to and from work, working thirteen and a half hours a day, seven days a week. My blood pressure was 160/106. I was ready to pop a cork, so to speak. My reprieve came when I was contacted by a recruiter who had a job in Florida working as a welding engineer/supervisor at the two-unit nuclear power plant in St. Lucie. It was a 20 percent pay increase and a whole new adventure. I took the job, and by Christmas 1985, we were in Florida, just in time to see BYU lose in the Citrus Bowl.

It was in Florida that I learned several important lessons. One of the first lessons I learned was that it's just as important to do things in a politically correct way as it is to do the right thing.

My first project was to revise welder testing. I created two tests where previously there had been ten tests. This was, of course, within my designated responsibilities, and it reduced the time welders were in the testing shop from three weeks to three days. It also reduced the weld failure rate from 9 percent to two-tenths of 1 percent.

Only highly qualified welders were able to pass the tests. The action saved the company about three million dollars a year. I thought I was a hero, but it created enemies of many managers and contractors who could no longer hire family and friends.

The second lesson I learned was that you never know where allegiances lie. I had an assistant who I could not tell what the individual was accomplishing. I had to redo everything the assistant did. The assistant's office was in the testing shop. At one point, I approached the shop foreman and asked him what the assistant did during work hours. The shop foreman didn't want to say anything, but I pressed the issue and was finally told that the assistant was trading stocks most of the day. By this time, I knew acting unilaterally was foolish. I had to be careful, so I assigned the assistant to work the night shift. Then I documented the mistakes and failures.

The assistant had been hired and paid by a contractor, so I took the information to my on-site manager. He in turn got the plant contractor manager involved who was furious. This individual happened to be one of the enemies I'd made with the welder-testing change. In time, and with several major mistakes made during his time on the night shift, the plant contractor was forced to lay off the assistant.

I thought "Good riddance," but then my corporate manager, who I reported to on technical matters, showed up at the plant with a series of questions. His weekly visits continued for nearly a year. Every week, he audited one of my major responsibilities.

It was an interesting time. Every time he left after his weekly audit, a whisper would tell me exactly what he would be auditing the coming week. I would then have the foreman and assistants spend the next week preparing for the upcoming week.

At one point, my corporate manager asked me, "Who's telling you when I'm coming and what I'll be looking at?"

"No one," I replied and told him I was just trying to do the right things.

It was only later that I learned the assistant who'd been fired had been mowing the lawns each week of my corporate manager, the department director, the previous site welding supervisor, and the plant contract managers. I had made another major mistake by not knowing where allegiances lay, and it cost me.

One of the things corporate had the nuclear welding employees do during non-plant outage time was to perform heat treating and supervisory functions at the fossil fuel power plants.

In the spring of 1989, I was working at the Port Everglades plant supervising the night shift during the repowering of one of the units. It was early morning, the sun had risen, and I was on top of one of the boilers about four hundred feet off the ground. I was tired and thinking of the beauty of the ocean. From where I stood, I could see ships and boats and even whales surfacing. I could see manatees in the river below. As I gazed upon the beauty of the scene, I began to daydream about cooking Dutch-oven potatoes and onions on a sagebrush fire. I knew it was time to head back west. I missed the mountains, valleys, and deserts. I enjoyed exploring places I hadn't lived before, and it had all been a great adventure, but this was not the place I truly loved and wanted to live. So I started to look for a new job in the west.

After several months, I was able to secure a position as a senior engineer with Kaiser Engineers at the Hanford Nuclear Site and moved my family to Benton City, Washington, just south of the Site. This was a much different job than I'd held before. It encompassed electrical, mechanical, civil, and chemical engineering.

Several areas on the site functioned like small towns with process plants and nuclear facilities. The engineers assigned to a particular area managed all repairs and new construction for that area. In addition to my area assignment, I had the responsibility of being the American Society of Mechanical Engineers (ASME) code engineer, which meant I had to ensure that applicable designs complied with the ASME code requirements and that those requirements were incorporated into company policies and procedures and the quality control programs. I was also responsible for preparing and hosting the ASME joint reviews and audits for the site.

This job was perfect for me because I worked from 7 a.m. to 4 p.m. Monday through Friday, with little to no overtime. Things at home weren't going well, and I needed to be there as often as possible to care for my children.

Not long after moving to Washington, I was faced with the reality of choosing between working a steady job or following my dream of becoming wealthy producing and marketing my inventions. As I often say, "It was a choice between my millions and my children." I considered my options. It would take at least five years to really make a go of my company. It would take all my time, energy, and focus. I would have to abandon spending time with my children.

At this time in my life, I was just coming to the realization that my children had suffered almost complete neglect while I wasn't home. I remember saying to myself, *I must be a great dad the way the kids glom onto me when I get home.* But it wasn't that I was a great father. It was the simple fact I was interacting with them and showing them attention. They needed me, and I wanted them to know I loved them and would be there for them.

So I made the decision to abandon my business plans and goals. Home life demanded every moment of my time, and I had to work to provide. Even when I was at work, home was not far from my thoughts. I had to call often to ensure things were okay at home and address any issues. It wasn't uncommon for me to leave work and rush home to resolve some crisis or another.

I stayed with the job for six years until the company offered a layoff package. I was what was known as a "protected entity" because I was a Vietnam-era veteran. This meant I wasn't likely to be laid off.

The company had just changed the manager of my group. The new manager was not actually an engineer but had been in law enforcement for most of his career. His persona and demeanor were one of an authoritarian and ultra-micromanager. He had no technical experience and didn't seem willing to listen to those with greater knowledge and experience.

I hadn't had any issues with him, but I knew it wouldn't be long before I did. To top that off, it was the last week of April 1995, and the Oklahoma City bombing had just taken place. Because of his law enforcement background, the new manager was particularly on edge and suspecting of everything and everyone. The prospect of working under this man's direction was the last thing I needed.

As I sat at my desk, I heard a whisper telling me that I should ask to be laid off. I followed the voice, and before long, I was home.

I was now certified in several environmental disciplines as well as welding and quality. With the help of the generous separation package, I decided to start a consulting business. I bought my first computer and printer and started working on creating the company.

Within a few days, my right wrist was in pain. It was the beginning of carpal tunnel issues. This pain was caused by the pressure of my wrist against the hard desk. In desperation, I knew I had to fix the situation. I had much to do, and my family needed me to support them.

There was foam rubber that came as packing material in one of the boxes. I cut a piece about six inches long and about an inch and a half square that fit under my wrist. It helped relieve the pain. The problem, however, was that I was doing graphic work that was better performed with less resistance on my wrist from the foam rubber. So I took a pair of scissors and cut the edges of the squared area, making it round. I'd just invented a rolling wrist support for use with a computer mouse. I enlisted the feedback of some friends who tried it out and reported back to me that they liked it.

I named this invention the Wally Roller and applied for a patent. I designed covers made from cotton linen in various patterns. Several friends from church owned serger sewing machines and could sew the covers for me. I ordered foam rubber made in 1 1/4 rounds that were eight feet long. We used scissors to cut the eight-foot lengths into six-inch lengths.

Figuring out how to get the foam rubber lengths into the covers was the next task. After several failures, the idea arose to use grilling tongs to compress the foam rubber lengths and insert them into cloth covers. It worked well, and I purchased five sets of tongs, and the kids and I sat watching TV and stuffing Wally Rollers. Artwork showing how to use the Wally Roller was created as well as packaging.

After contacting several office supply businesses, over five thousand dollars of Wally Rollers were sold. Shortly after this success, the US Patient Office sent a letter denying the Wally Roller patient application. Someone had already been granted a patent for a rolling wrist support that had three padded roller rods set in a frame. It was a bit cumbersome and wasn't on the market. As a result, the production and marketing of the Wally Roller came to a stop. I still have a case in storage.

It wasn't just the possible patent infringement that had me suspending production and marketing; it was also being home and seeing how the children were being treated and neglected. I had become convinced that something had to be done. As before, I realized I couldn't pursue the creation of new businesses. I started looking for employment. It was a challenging task. I was earning a good salary, and finding employment commensurate with my past salary was going to take time.

I started working with Hanford Employment Resource Center, which was included in the severance package provided with the layoff. I made a goal of submitting 125 applications and résumés a week for the first month then twenty-five a week until I secured employment.

It wasn't long before the money ran out. I met with my church leader and asked for help, which was given. The church leaders met with me, determined the family's needs, and made a food and commodity order to assure my family had what was needed. I then did every task the church asked and even requested more things to do. I was able to repair a widow's stock fence damaged during a flood. Each week, I was asked to work at the bishop's storehouse. I was assigned to put food and commodities orders together for families in eastern Washington receiving assistance, which included my own family.

I had expected to have more prospects than I had at the time. One day, on my way home from working at the storehouse, I was praying. Once again, it was more begging than praying. As I was doing my begging prayer, I heard the Spirit say to me, "Be patient. I am blessing you."

My thoughts turned to the food and commodities I had in the back of the vehicle. I couldn't have purchased higher quality food. There were no steaks, but there were roasts and hamburger and everything from bread to butter and jam. I was doing everything I could to secure employment and doing any and all assignments given to me. I thought about how when I was employed, I was blessed. Now that I was unemployed and not self-sufficient, I was still being blessed. I knew I needed to be patient and faithful and that it would all work out.

One year almost to the day after my layoff, I found a job in Evanston, Wyoming, with Elkhorn Construction. I was hired as a manager and was responsible for training, quality, and human relations functions. During the approximately six years I was employed with Elkhorn, we were able to create an accredited and certified craft-training program for electricians, millwrights, carpenters, pipe fitters, insulators, and welders. We also developed project management courses for managers and supervisors. Additionally, we published a quarterly newsletter, *The Elkhorn Bugle*, for five and a half years, which we shared with employees and customers.

In 2002, I was given an opportunity to return to work in the electrical power-generating industry. I secured a position with Entergy in The Woodlands, Texas. I was a senior lead engineer and the subject-matter expert on welding, metallurgy, nondestructive testing, and ASME code work and processes, as well as high-energy piping. During the time I worked with Entergy—and while attending many seminars identifying and locating the service damage mechanisms power plant piping can experience during operation—I noticed there was no information on how to manage the information discovered.

After gaining a complete understanding of the cause and effects of the service damage mechanisms, I began to create a management system that identified and ranked by score the welds and locations that were most likely to experience service damage. This approach allowed the budgeting and the focus of resources where it was most advisable.

In 2007, a position similar to that I'd held with Entergy came available with PacifiCorp/Rocky Mountain Power in Utah. I applied and was offered the position. I had wanted to return to Utah all my career, and this was it. My mother and stepfather were now elderly, and I felt I should be close to them so I could help them as needed.

During my time with PacifiCorp, I created a weld and component ranking system that assured the high-energy piping operated safely and reliably. We were able to identify and repair all service damage before catastrophically failing, causing personnel injury or plant damage. The program provided the ability to update the rankings with evaluation and inspection results. This update then provided a new set of welds and locations to evaluate and inspect. With four years between inspections, we could provide plants with projected estimates, giving them time to plan and budget for the next inspections.

In April 2020, I retired from PacifiCorp and then consulted for three years. I had a successful and fulfilling forty-one-year career in the power plant industry.

Except for the time I served God, I had worked from the age of fourteen to sixty-eight. I had been blessed with safety, health, and challenging lucrative employment. I invented several inspection tools and created systems and programs that continue to help manage critical plant equipment and issues. I had been published in a professional journal. Now I have written this book.

I have found in life that it is much easier to look back than to look forward. I could have never imagined many of the things I've learned or accomplished. I started out life as poor as anyone could be, without anything but dim hope and a naive dream. I was filled with ignorance, insecurity, and fear. I have experienced heart-wrenching failures in relationships and marriage. There were times I was faithless, disobedient, and rebellious. I am deeply disappointed in myself for those times.

I had a lot to learn and a great deal of self-discipline to develop. I feel I should have been more faithful and trusting of God. I had to learn to love myself as well as others. I have come to realize that I cannot accomplish all the hopes and dreams I have for my family.

Many of those hopes and dreams can only be accomplished by my children and their children.

The one thing for which I am certain is we are being blessed in our efforts, and as always, "We're getting better."

The End